Using
Instructional
Media
Effectively

USING
INSTRUCTIONAL
MEDIA
EFFECTIVELY

by JACK TANZMAN
and
KENNETH J. DUNN

PARKER PUBLISHING COMPANY, INC.   West Nyack, N.Y.

LIBRARY OF CONGRESS
CATALOG CARD NUMBER: 78–135020

PRINTED IN THE UNITED STATES OF AMERICA

ISBN–0–13–939652–7
B & P

About the Authors

Jack Tanzman is Regional Director of the Nassau County ESEA Title III Center and is also Director of Research and Development for the Board of Cooperative Educational Services, Nassau County, New York.

He was formerly the Director of Educational Communications for the Plainview–Old Bethpage Public Schools, Plainview, New York. He is media consultant to *School Management* Magazine, preparing a column, and serves as a consultant to school districts, colleges, and architectural firms.

In 1963–64, Mr. Tanzman directed the federally sponsored study of educational communications centers. Since then, he has lectured on the center concept throughout the United States.

Mr. Tanzman has taught in public school systems on the elementary and secondary levels. He developed and directed work-study programs and assisted in writing dissemination guidelines for the U.S. Office of Education.

He holds a B.A. and an M.S. from N.Y.U. and has completed post master's work at Columbia and Johns Hopkins Universities.

Kenneth J. Dunn is Superintendent of Schools, Chappaqua, New York, and Adjunct Professor at Hunter College, New York. He is the former Deputy Superintendent of Schools for the Board of Cooperative Educational Services (BOCES) in Nassau County and Executive Director of THE EDUCATION COUNCIL for School Research and Development (TEC). He also served as Director of the county's ESEA Title III Regional Center. Formerly, he was Superintendent of Schools in Leonia, New Jersey. Dr. Dunn has coordinated national conferences and has designed and implemented a variety of educational programs. He has published several articles on human and management relations, administration, personnel policies, and curriculum.

Dr. Dunn also has coauthored several books including *Visuals Into Words* and *A Quest for Questions* (New York: AEVAC, Inc., 1969).

He holds a B.A. degree from Hunter College and M.A. and Ed.D. degrees from Teachers College, Columbia University.

Foreword

In prehistoric times, according to a current comic strip, someone scratched a diagram on the wall of a cave and said to his audience, "See, it's round; let's call it a wheel; it may be useful someday."

Centuries later there was chalk and then the book copied by scribes. Five centuries ago there was movable type, and only a century ago there were daguerreotypes of the Civil War. And with the coming of electricity there followed in something less than quick succession—indeed, at about the rate of one invention per generation—the moving picture, radio, television, and the computer.

In the meantime, back at the schoolhouse there is the chalk, the book, maybe the moving picture and radio, possibly television, and a computer here and there.

With life getting increasingly technical and electrical, and with the medium ready for the message, education is still struggling with instructional technology. There is, obviously, an urgent need for better answers to such questions as the following:

1. Can the library embrace all the carriers of information under single management, or must libraries be mostly for books while audiovisual support is provided from another dispensary?

2. Can software keep pace with hardware? Already we have boxes that can talk but have nothing to say.

3. Can we avoid the institutional desire to find a single and universal

5

solution? Will some schools be free to travel the route of "hands on" materials while others deliver information from a central source?

4. How do we cement the relations between the teacher and the supplier of devices and programs so that whatever comes into the school from the outside to speed learning will be cast as teacher-extender rather than teacher-replacement? Clearly the teacher possesses the territory: he welcomes extension but takes a dim view of replacement.

Whatever one's philosophy, if there is the desire to capitalize on all the ways that relevant and vivid information can be transmitted, the means are at hand and they are within our grasp economically. The report to the President and Congress of the United States by the Commission on Instructional Technology makes the case and issues the call.

This book deals with the practicable—the things we can do now. It has useful things to say to schools just getting started and to those well on the way.

> HAROLD B. GORES
> President
> Educational Facilities Laboratories, Inc.
> Non-Profit Corp. established by the Ford Foundation

The Scope and Purpose of This Book...

The objective of this work is to provide practical solutions to the problems administrators face when attempting improved learning through more effective use of teaching media. It begins by analyzing major instructional problems as they actually are, listing specific teaching-learning situations which need improvement (whether it be the upgrading of ineffective, older classrooms or the design of flexible teaching zones in new buildings), and follows these by pinpointing the essential considerations and suggested *action* procedures the reader can apply. The total introduction of changes in teaching media is considered in a way that will provide tested guidelines, checklists, designs, tips, and cautions to insure that the proposed change will be desirable and effective when instituted. The material goes far beyond the mere "audiovisual aids" aspect of improving teaching and learning.

For example, some of those old, inflexible "Washington School" classrooms can be converted into modern, fully equipped multimedia teaching centers. Portable teaching walls with split rear-screen projection can speed the adoption of effective team teaching or large-group instruction in old buildings. Administrators and staff who are planning new buildings are given criteria for design, plans for learning zones and equipment, placement and usage, and suggestions for staff involvement, effective student scheduling and staff deployment. Among the specific guidelines to upgrade your instructional program you will find ways to establish teacher resource centers, start audiovisual programs in elementary schools, and obtain and utilize funds for training your staff.

7

The scope of teaching media is broad, and the opportunities for improved learning enormous. The field is undergoing such an explosive expansion, it is becoming increasingly difficult to focus on the practical forms of media that offer greatest potential in situations similiar to your own. That is the purpose of this book, and the material is based on actual experience. The procedures have been measured by professional evaluation methods, and only the significant, most productive results have been used as a basis for the material that follows.

The authors believe that effective solutions and improvements require close collaboration between teachers and administrators. They have, therefore, integrated the analysis of problems, guidelines for change, and action procedures for schools into a pattern which requires joint teacher-administrative effort and mutual support to use teaching media more effectively.

JACK TANZMAN
KENNETH J. DUNN

Acknowledgments

Special thanks to James E. Doherty and Paul Abramson, both former editors of SCHOOL MANAGEMENT Magazine, for their assistance in the preparation of the monthly columns utilized for this book.

The authors also are indebted to a number of friends and professionals who aided in the completion of this book. Among those who made major contributions through their professional advice, suggestions, encouragement, editing and correcting were:

William Brubaker—The Perkins & Will Partnership, Architects
Lee Campion—New York State Education Department
Paul Cleaves—Bailey Film Associates
Rita Stafford Dunn—St. John's University
Morton C. Gassman—State University of New York at Albany
Harold Gores—Educational Facilities Laboratories, Inc.
Alan C. Green—Educational Facilities Laboratories, Inc.
Ronald T. Lau—Board of Cooperative Educational Services
Margaret J. Reddy—The Education Council
John Shaver—Shaver & Company, Architects

Contents

Using
Instructional
Media
Effectively

1

Building the Foundation
for an Effective
Instructional Program

There Ought to Be a Place: Key Objectives
in Building a Practical Media Program

One enlightened teacher stated a fundamental principle of change for the better this way, "I prefer to work with teachers and administrators who are *dissatisfied*. They're *unhappy* with their own achievement as educators and continually seek to improve the act of instruction."

Staff members who search for better techniques of teaching are not the complainers and "gripers"; they are out scouring the used book stores to find illustrations, devices and even "magic" tricks which will motivate learning and aid the discovery process in teaching science; they are poring over catalogs to order manipulative materials for building mathematics concepts and skills; they are writing and reproducing special materials for slow and advanced readers; they are seeking original source materials to build bridges between the realities of past and present political history; and they are ordering equipment to build villages, cities and their environments in order to demonstrate principles of sociology, anthropology, economics, and ecology. The teachers and administrators who apply pressure on the front office or the board of education for the "stuff of learning" are usually the ones who want to improve teaching and learning. Those staffs who continually plead, "There ought to be a place . . ." are most likely to obtain the teachers' resource rooms, the instructional materials corners, and the media centers.[1]

Indeed, "there ought to be a place . . ." should be printed at the top of a blank sheet of paper and circulated among the faculty as one way to produce a list of the key objectives to be considered in building a practical media center.

One such practical media center was derived from the recommendations of 2,000 classroom teachers on a questionnaire distributed by the Nassau County ESEA Title III Regional Center. *There Ought to Be a Place,* therefore, can provide an operating definition of a media center in action—as envisioned by its chief customers, the teachers.

There ought to be a place:

- where overhead projectuals, audio and video tapes, activity sheets, units, dioramas, and other instructional materials can be designed by teachers, scholars, technicians, and students to meet individual and group needs;

- where teachers and administrators can call for information, pamphlets, magazines, books, news articles, research studies, materials and other resources and have their requests filled in twenty-four hours;

- that demonstrates and helps to adapt innovations and effective techniques in the classroom; e.g., teaching walls, teaching desks, and multiple projection and sound presentations (see chapters 2 and 7);

- that will evaluate local curricula and work with the staff to develop improved and relevant courses and materials;

- that will use all of the local and regional resources available—libraries, museums, cultural groups, government, industry, colleges and universities, and the community—in effective and meaningful patterns;

- where scholars and professionals in residence, e.g., poets, writers, musicians, scientists, and economists, can work with students and teachers;

- that develops materials and techniques for slow learners, the disadvantaged and the handicapped as well as for average and advanced students;

---

[1] In the authors' view, teachers' resource centers and instructional materials centers are synonymous with media centers only if they include all of the staffing, equipment, facilities, and materials needed for providing an outstanding instructional program. (See chapters 2, 3 and 6.)

- where teachers can receive training and skills in developing and using all media to improve instruction; and
- that will provide continuing consultation and resources to teachers, students, and administrators whether in the classrooms, the media center or the community.

Photo 1. Taped television programs are channeled upon request. (Photograph courtesy of Lee E. Campion, Director, Division of Educational Communications, New York State Education Department.)

Photo 2. Students check out multimedia lessons that include filmstrips, tapes, and student response sheets from the librarian. (Photograph courtesy of Mt. San Jacinto College, Gilman Hot Springs, California.)

Photo 3. A sound technician makes multiple copies of each taped lesson. (Photograph courtesy of Mt. San Jacinto College, Gilman Hot Springs, California.)

Photo 4. Films are indexed and shelved for immediate availability to teacher or student. (Bell & Howell, Audio Visual Products Division, Chicago, Illinois.)

How to Get Started: Selecting What You Need— and Can Use Effectively

The media center would become quite a place, indeed, if all of the objectives developed under "There Ought to Be a Place" were met completely. These objectives could form the foundation for a media center and program that would raise the level of instruction significantly in a building or district. The media program, of course, includes all of the process elements—the procedures, activities and experiences described above. One way to begin is to establish a collaborative team of teachers and administrators to list realistic goals upon which to develop a media program for your building. Obviously, a media program is not possible without equipment and materials. Just having instructional materials, however, does not mean that you have a *program*.

Districts that want to develop good media programs should start by "thinking small." How small? How much is needed to get started without considering space and staff at this point? (See chapter 3.)

Unfortunately, there are no easy answers. We can, however, provide certain guidelines that may be used by either a wealthy or economically disadvantaged school or district.

Further, it must be acknowledged that no media program can be developed without some minimum expenditures. Perhaps we can begin with an approximate estimate of $5 per pupil. This amount does, not imply that a school or a district must seek "new money," for the median district in the United States is spending $5.14 per elementary school pupil on media materials, supplies, salaries, and equipment.[2] Only twenty-five per cent of the nation's schools are spending less than $3.03 per pupil.

Five dollars per pupil per year, in the average elementary school of 500 students, would provide a financial foundation of $2,500. How might that amount be used productively? (The guidelines suggested here could be used for a district or a school, whether you had $1,000 or $5,000 and 300 pupils or 10,000 pupils.)

The first step, logically, must be to inventory the equipment (hardware) and materials (software) already owned by the school. Record players, a fair supply of records, and projectors are usually available in most schools. Once a staff knows what it has at its disposal it is almost ready to start spending the allotted $2,500. Before requisitions are written, remember three basic principles:

1. Start by buying what teachers can best use now, not the latest gadget on the market. With just $2,500 available, this principle is fairly easy to follow and applies whether you have $500 or $15,000 to spend.

---

[2] "The Cost of Audio-Visual Instruction, 1970–71," *School Management* (October, 1970), p. 26.

Teachers can *use* record players, motion picture projectors, slide, film-strip and overhead projectors, and other simple machines. Most teachers already know *how* to operate all but the motion picture projector. (If teachers do not know how, children frequently do!) Those who do not have the knowledge can be trained in a relatively short period of time. Furthermore, most teachers also know *what* to do with these tools in a classroom.

2. Insure that you have enough materials to go with your equipment. There is no point in purchasing four motion picture projectors if you have just four films to show. It would be wiser to purchase just one projector this year and a number of usable—and reusable—films. You may also wish to consider renting films and/or a lease-purchase arrangement for both films and equipment. Consider several estimates and do some comparison shopping.

3. Do not try to develop a complete school media program in one year on a limited budget. Concentrate your activities each year on a single type of equipment and its related materials. Thus, you might buy an overhead projector and commercially prepared transparencies and materials for teacher use the first year. If teachers need training in the use of overhead transparencies, begin with equipment and materials with which they are familiar. Later, schedule workshops in the use of overhead projectors and budget for their purchase the second year. Commercial companies would be happy to assist you.

It really does not matter in which direction you start. It is essential that you realize your first year's program is just a start. You should plan an overall buying program spread over many years so that you are able to concentrate on equipping each phase of the media program when teachers are ready to use the specific equipment and materials effectively.

One planned program, for the first year, might include record players, if you do not already have them available. These would be very important at the elementary school level because they may be used in so many activities that basically reinforce a variety of curriculum areas.

Assuming you already have record players or similar "basic" tools, the acquisition of any of the equipment and materials mentioned earlier would be a proper second step. (Maps and globes are not suggested in this discussion because many districts purchase these under different sections of the budget. Further, elementary school buildings are usually well stocked with these items. Consideration of programing better ways of using maps and globes is usually a prerequisite to obtaining them.)

Overhead and filmstrip projectors are a sound investment. Both of these tools are extremely easy to use, there is a wide range of commercial transparencies and filmstrips available, and the materials themselves are inexpensive when compared with some others. Motion picture projectors are more expensive and, in some ways, more difficult to use effectively, although the proper use of films offers excellent teaching opportunities not otherwise available. (See chapter 7.)

No matter which type of equipment you choose for your "starter set," you are going to have to add to it on a consistent basis for many years before you have a really adequate arsenal of equipment and materials. Do not forget that what you purchase must be used effectively in the classroom; this is the key to the start of a fine media program.

Tailoring the Kind and Amount of Equipment for the Teacher and the Learner: Three Prescriptions

The editor of a local newspaper asked a challenging question. "Thirty years ago," he said, "a typical student in a typical classroom sat at a desk with an inkwell; he used a textbook, some paper, a pen or pencil, and he sat behind a girl whose pigtails could be dipped into the inkwell—if the teacher wasn't looking. What occurs today? Describe the present-day typical classroom with its teaching machines, overhead projectors, television, and technological gadgets."

We started to name all of the newer equipment—most of it of the "audiovisual" variety that is so well known. Midway through this exercise it became apparent that we were not describing today's typical classroom. We were outlining a very idealistic situation that exists in very few school districts.

Think about it. How does the typical classroom of today differ from one that existed thirty years ago? The desk is probably movable now; so is the chair. Ball-point pens have replaced the inkwell, and fewer girls have pigtails (which almost renders the inkwell unnecessary, if not obsolete).

Other than a few physical changes, what is really different? The basic tools are still the textbook, paper, pencil, or pen; the teacher usually stands at the front of the room and writes on the board, talks to or "at" the class, begins discussions, and occasionally establishes reading or work groups.

A student may see a few movies or filmstrips today not available in the thirties. He may even attend a large-group meeting or be exposed to television once in a while. When you examine specifics, however, the typical classroom situation today is little different from the classroom of thirty years ago, despite the publicity given to the newer teaching tools and techniques. With the exception of more windows and better furnishings, the typical "modern" classroom remains unchanged!

Wonderful media tools do exist, but the fact that they exist does not mean that they are being used in classrooms.

Why? Or, why not?

There are a number of answers that could be given to this question.

Lack of money is one. It simply costs too much to equip classrooms with all of the available media. There are ways to get started, of course, and some of these were discussed in the previous section.

Perhaps even more important questions are "Why use media at all?" and "Were not the methods of the thirties successful?"

The answers are obvious but bear repeating. Society is in a state of rapid change and turmoil. The knowledge and communication explosions require teaching techniques which utilize the very technology born of this age of growth. Media in the form of television, movies, still photography and radio bombard our educable youth night and day. Thus, media are relevant to youth and provide the tools both to retain and transmit knowledge and to teach skills far more effectively than by lecture or question and answer. Then, too, we must reach more students with more problems for longer periods than ever before. Media can aid in teaching all of them.

Teachers and students are individuals with individual skills, abilities and potentials. Media tools can allow all to teach and learn according to those abilities. Moreover, the students of today are more sophisticated, more involved, and more demanding of exposure to reality. Media can bring the real world into their learning experiences.

Finally, media can (1) stimulate learning through the appeal to multiple senses; (2) provide for individual differences; (3) be programed for independent learning; (4) be utilized for varying school organizational patterns and learning groups of different sizes; (5) bring the sight and sound of unreachable places and experiences to all; (6) establish rapport and self-teaching control; and (7) provide immediacy, delayed retrieval and use away from the classroom.

Tailoring to your particular staff the kind and amount of media purchased is another problem. Sometimes we speak of individual and group differences among students and forget to apply the same principle to our staffs when we are administrators and to our supervisors and fellow faculty members when we are teachers. Some important organizational and human relations prescriptions apply whether you are tailoring a suit, a dress or a program to an individual or group. If these prescriptions are not followed, the suit (or program) will not fit well. If it does not make us feel comfortable, we will not wear (use) it. Let us examine these prescriptions.

1. The Problem of Change: Lack of Relevance and Reward

You cannot force a bold, plaid jacket on a Madison Avenue executive accountant who always wears pin-stripes; nor can you make a woman change her hair style, unless she's motivated by reasons that seem real and rewarding to her, such as gaining a more youthful appearance or maintaining a fashionable one.

Similarly, teachers are not prepared to use what is already available, particularly in the area of the new technology. They don't know how to operate the "terrible gadgets," or they've been frustrated too often by mechanical breakdowns. Sometimes they cannot get what they need when they want it. More frequently, teachers simply do not want to try to use the newer media. And principals are so harassed with day-to-day "front-line" problems that they understandably are reluctant to add new burdens to themselves or to their staffs.

Too often media supervisors do not provide the kind of leadership needed to encourage teachers to explore media resources. Even in those districts that can afford to buy enough equipment to establish media programs; the programs do not really develop. The equipment may be placed in the control of a media director who too often turns out to be more of a "tinkerer than a thinkerer" and facilitator. "Audiovisual" becomes his private domain, and the emphasis is placed almost entirely on *things* rather than *people* developing *programs*.

The teacher can easily become the forgotten ingredient. Districts now discuss "systems"—TV systems, communications systems. They also explore multimedia and cross-media "packages." Decision makers spend their time looking at more and more technical equipment. The fact that the teacher cannot use it, will not use it, or does not know how to use it is often ignored.

Of course, this is not true everywhere. Some districts and some schools *do* develop good programs and consider and involve the teacher. In too many cases, however, the "equipment first" philosophy reigns. If you attend any media convention you will probably hear a great deal of discussion about random-interlace, orthicon, vidicon, automatic storage and retrieval, and the systems approach—but almost nothing about how to help "Miss Jones" make use of filmstrips in the teaching of reading or the use of overhead transparencies to teach social studies.

The key concern in the further development—and use—of media in the schools is Miss Jones. Unless *she uses* it, the most advanced equipment in the world is absolutely useless.

Rx: "Try on" some media before purchasing. Look in the mirror of Miss Jones' perceptions as you begin to change "accessories." Have her witness some expert "tailors" demonstrating the use of the new "garments" and the functions that the accessories serve when the new equipment is "worn." Let a teachers' group work together on selection, use, orientation and demonstrations. Above all, consider the wishes and reactions of the individual *teacher-consumer* at all times as she learns of the advantages and rewards of effective teaching with media. To produce an even more effective program, encourage Miss Jones to introduce some interested *students* to the demonstration-selection process!

2. *The Problem of Timing: Lack of Training and Readiness*

Technology leads practice in so many sectors of our nation's life. Media technology, too, has soared way ahead of utilization. The problem of developing realistic and economically feasible media programs in the schools is often one of timing and training. We must remember that we would not expect the average automobile operator to know how to drive a rocket to Mars without exposure to an intensive training sequence. Perhaps the analogy is severely drawn, but the unknown in media equipment might seem just as forbidding to an elementary teacher as launching herself to the moon.

Rx: Start with what the teacher can use in the classroom now—just one step beyond the chalkboard and the textbook. Start at the beginning and build up to the use of sophisticated equipment, rather than the other way around. In other words, plan one step at a time. This approach will allow a teacher to move to the more complex machines when he or she can really use them—when timing and training integrate.

3. *The Problem of Apathy: Lack of Momentum*

"We don't have enough equipment to go around. What's the best way to use what we have?" This is a common question, but far too little thought is given to the answer. If you have a single tape recorder or motion picture projector for a building, a simple solution is to keep it in some central place and let teachers use it when and as they wish.

This approach is acceptable, provided that enough teachers actually remember where the equipment is located, know how to get it when they need it, know how to use it once they have it, and are knowledgeable about the materials to use with it.

Unfortunately, the equipment is often deposited in the school office or storage area and forgotten except, possibly, for its use at the annual PTA dinner and dance. Inertia and apathy make media the "wallflowers" of the school.

Rx: Open the store. Recently, a number of media directors, superintendents and principals advocated a new approach to this problem. Instead of storing the equipment and supplies in the principal's office or custodian's closet—where it is supposedly at the disposal of all teachers (but used by few or none)—why not select a single teacher and let him have all the equipment in his room at all times? He would have his own "media store."

Now, instead of having a number of teachers provide their students with an unsatisfactory smattering of media-aided education, one teacher, at least, could really prepare and present an organized program.

Moreover, if you have chosen the right entrepreneur for the store—and if you give him the administrative support he needs—he will soon become the focus of media education in the building. He will be able to prepare programs and outlines; he will assist other teachers; and he'll become a working "expert" on the use of media in the classroom.

Of course, there are some dangers in this course of action. You cannot remove all media tools from the other teachers. If you have only one projector in the building, all teachers must have access to it. You may still "store" the projector with a selected teacher. Do not make him responsible for it, however. He should be a teacher, not a mechanic or a clerk.

Another danger is that the teacher will become a "principal's pet," as obnoxious to the other teachers as a "teacher's pet" is to other pupils. This, however, is an administrative problem that may be overcome through proper leadership and the perceptive selection of a status teacher.

By selecting one teacher and giving him an opportunity to show by example how much can be done in a single classroom, you will create demand among the other teachers for an equal opportunity. And that is the point at which you can act to spread the media program.

The public is naturally reluctant to spend large amounts on inactive equipment that is on display but not used in the building. Once teachers have demonstrated how these tools can be used and have started demanding them for themselves, however, an atmosphere is created whereby boards of education and administrators can obtain the necessary financial support.

One media leader in a school may accomplish more in one term than all the equipment in the world merely stored in a principal's office. Once the store is open and the window is filled with displays, customers will inevitably sample the products, and the advantages of media education may now become available to all pupils.

Developing Your Own Media Materials: Some Cautions

Back in the early thirties, and during World War II, it was not uncommon to see a man with a tobacco pouch and cigarette paper "rolling his own." If the man was skillful and had the "knack" he could save money this way.

Of course, the idea of rolling one's own cigarettes fell out of vogue as more and more people found that they could not do the job as well or as quickly as machines. In addition, even the cost of materials eventually exceeded that of "ready-mades."

Many media programs are in that same "roll-your-own" category right now when it comes to materials. Some media materials obviously cannot be made by teachers. It is rather difficult to make a usable sound film, or even a filmstrip, unless you have professional know-how. Many schools and school districts take a different view, however, when it comes to projectuals for overhead and opaque projectors and tapes for language laboratories. Administrators assume that these may be made by any teacher.

While a few teachers can indeed prepare excellent transparencies, any teacher can and should develop bulletin board displays, story boards and other simple instructional materials. For the most part, however, having teachers make their own specialized types of media materials is a step in the wrong direction. Despite the argument that teachers and students should prepare transparencies because this gives them the opportunities to create and "do" instead of passively watching, the net gain is questionable.

In the first place, few teachers have the talent to do the job properly. There is little that is worse in teaching than working with inferior materials. It is better to forego completely the use of the equipment than to use it to display ineffective, poorly prepared materials.

In the second place, a great deal of a teacher's time (of necessity) must be involved. At a time when we are planning to use teacher aides and instructional secretaries to relieve teachers of clerical and technical tasks, it is inappropriate to suggest that the trend should be reversed when it comes to preparing media materials.

Photo 5. An illustrator uses rough story board illustrations to produce finished color illustrations for multimedia lessons. (Photograph courtesy of Mt. San Jacinto College, Gilman Hot Springs, California.)

In the third place, making your own projectuals and other media materials is expensive. It is expensive in terms of the equipment needed, the materials that are wasted by amateurs, and in the time consumed that might be better spent *designing and planning the use of media materials for instructional purposes. Graphics technicians and media specialists usually can translate teaching ideas into prepared media materials far more effectively than teachers can.* Each professional would then be functioning properly in the area of his own competence, training and creativity. Teacher and student "doing" would be increased in the area of design; creation is in the act of conceiving, not laboriously (and often poorly) translating the concept onto film transparencies. An analogy might be to request a successful novelist to set his own type and to run a printing press in order to produce his own book.

There are, however, certain conditions and reasons for a school to prepare its own materials. The decision to create your own instructional materials depends upon some basic criteria dealing with cost, ability, space, need, and appropriate function. Here are some basic criteria:

1. In general, unless a district uses media extensively and often, it is less expensive to buy prepared projectuals and tapes than to make them yourself.

2. If you need special projectuals or materials that do not exist on the commercial market, or if you require a large amount of media materials, you also need an expert technician or graphics clerk to do the work. He should be a professional who works with the teachers' ideas. This technician need not be employed full time but should be available on a regular schedule.

3. It is possible to have a graphics clerk work in a central district office, but it would be advantageous to the teachers and the clerk if work space could be provided in each school. This space need not be elaborate, although some equipment is needed and a dark room is useful. Ideally it should be located in a teacher's room, a corner of the administrative offices where typewriters and copying equipment might be available, or in a library, if space in the other areas is not available.

4. Be certain that you have valid educational reasons for preparing your own materials. In view of the previous cautions raised, the most important questions for teachers and administrators to answer include these: Why are we producing our own materials? Do they serve a specific instructional or behavioral objective? Do commercial materials exist that will serve instructional needs as well or better than "do-it-yourself" creations? Might the time and energy expended developing media materials be spent more profitably with students, with technical aides, or in evaluating commercial materials? Obviously, if you have invented a transparency or technique that

Photo 6. A graphics specialist translates a teaching idea into a media presentation. (Photograph courtesy of Amo DeBernardis, President, Portland Community College, Portland, Oregon.)

serves a unique purpose you have fulfilled a teaching goal, and perhaps your creation should be submitted to a commercial publisher for wider dissemination. The techniques for the proper preparation and use of media such as overhead projectuals are well established and based on sound teaching and learning theory. It is a rare teacher who combines experience, creativity and technical know-how in creating a superior transparency. Indeed, even many commercial publishers have missed the mark in reproducing maps that cannot be read; in placing material on relatively expensive overhead projectuals, when less costly 2 × 2 slides would have served the same purpose; in not utilizing overlay techniques for motivation, interest, and proper teaching sequence; and in not researching materials with teachers and students.

5. Finally, the teaching functions of planning, designing and evaluating media and techniques should supersede mechanical and technical functions, unless the teacher's creativity is so great, the need so pressing and the lack of technical assistance so critical that the teacher must complete the task. In general, assigning teachers to this type of teaching function is a fading practice.

Evaluation: A Checklist for Building on the Results

Nearly everyone agrees that programs, facilities and materials should be evaluated and that evaluation should improve instruction. There is little agreement, however, about what constitutes *good* evaluation.

Too often evaluation is based on unrelated, rambling questions with little opportunity for planning improvement. For example:

1. Are teachers using instructional film in all subject areas or just a few—social studies, language arts, etc.?

2. Are *all* teachers making use of educational trips?

3. Are individual teachers using the great variety of materials available?

Answers to these questions would provide little true evaluation and practically no useful information for improvement. The first question establishes an emotional bias in the observer and the observed. Furthermore, it does not examine the learner, the way the film is being used, the motivation, the achievement, the quality of the film, its appropriateness to the curriculum, or its relevance for the students. The second and third questions also ignore methods of teaching or the results; they are more concerned with the operational techniques. Moreover, most sets of haphazard questions such as these fail to consider relative values, i.e., the *weight* or *strength* of a particular standard. For example, the consistent and effective use of a variety of media materials by a teacher might be assigned more importance than her ability to operate all of the equipment. A single field trip to a museum that shows film classics *might* have greater impact on students than weekly showings from the local film library center.

Another evaluation trap is the establishment of opposites or dichotomies, e.g., product vs. process; tests and measurements vs. teacher perceptions; and objective description vs. subjective judgment. It should be obvious that all of these evaluation items, and more, may be needed to improve instruction. We must measure results and products, but how they were achieved may become all-important in making recommendations for program changes. Statistics, data, experiments, and designs are necessary elements of the scientific method, but chance, non-measurable human interactions and other factors of the human experience must be considered as well—none should be excluded. Finally, judgment would seem to be valueless without description.

Therefore, three major categories are suggested for media program evaluation. Relative values and assigned weights of importance should be considered by the staff (and consultants, if used) at the time the evaluation design and its objectives are developed. The three categories are:

1. *Operation*—questions that deal with the quality and efficiency of the structure and operation of the project, e.g., administration, scheduling, staff, facilities, and coordination.
2. *Process*—questions that deal with the day-to-day and month-to-month effects of the program, the numbers of people involved and how they are affected, and consideration of appraisals as a means to improve the program.
3. *Product*—questions that deal with measurable results in quantitative and qualitative terms; generalizations about the fulfillment of your needs and appraisals of how these needs were met.
   a. *Operation*
      1) Was the project established and the program initiated in the time period contemplated?
      2) Were the in-service sessions and workshops sufficient to orient teachers and administrators so that they could use the equipment?
      3) Were the chief program and staff problems identified, and what steps were taken to improve remaining areas of concern or to improve the operation or structure of the media program?
      4) Were effective and usable materials, e.g., films, filmstrips, and transparencies, cataloged and annotated for easy accessibility? Were these items correlated with print materials?
      5) What were the chief facility and scheduling problems, and how could they be solved?
   b. *Process*
      1) How many teachers and students are affected by the program, make use of the media, initiate new activities or materials, and act on results?
      2) Which commercial media are provided to improve instruction? How are they used?
      3) Which media achieve the most positive results? How is this determined?
      4) How are successful media techniques and products demonstrated and implemented? What modifications in the procedures are necessary and why?
      5) How is their impact or contribution measured?
      6) What criteria are developed and modified in selecting media? How are they developed? What improvements can be made?
      7) How are developed materials and activities structured into the program? What provisions are made for long-term evaluation?
      8) What are the procedures for involving teachers and students in

the development and improvement of these media and their use?

c. *Product*

1) What generalizations can be made about the program, its services and its effect on those who use it?

2) Do the materials and activities meet the needs of teachers and students?

3) Are the media sought by teachers and students? What analysis can be made of the reasons offered for enthusiastic reception, cautions, optimism, apathy, or rejection?

4) What techniques and instruments were employed to evaluate the media before and after their use in the program?

5) What verification can be established for the data collected, interpreted and reported?

6) Are there plans for thorough study of the materials, training activities, and the ultimate impact on students and the school program? How will the product be measured?

7) To what extent do teachers utilize the materials and services of the program? Are they utilizing the media properly in the classrooms? Effectively?

8) Are attitudes, programs, perceptions and decisions affected by the program? Which ones? To what degree? For which positive ends?

How to Provide Continuing Education Programs for Administration and Staff

Although chapter 4 will describe in-service programs in more detail, consideration should be given here to some of the types of continuing education projects that can aid in building the foundations of an effective instructional program through the improved use of media. There are at least four training program prototypes that have excellent chances for changing behavioral patterns and improving instruction.

1. *Administrative Clinics*

Establish clinics in your building or district for administrators, supervisors, grade chairmen, department chairmen, team leaders, or any personnel who have responsibility for assisting teachers to improve the teaching-learning process.

Maintain an unstructured approach. Schedule only as many meetings as are needed. Allow the course to flow in true clinic style; the answers and activities should be based on the needs and concerns expressed by the administrators. The consultant who operates the clinic must be prepared for such questions as "What do I look for when I observe a media lesson, e.g., overhead projectuals, film or a slide presentation?" "How do I help a teacher to do a more effective job with continuous film loops and projectors?" "How do I evaluate all of the materials and equipment that are listed by the media industry?"

The group should structure itself in addition to observing some answers and guidelines. Practicing what they learn will aid the clinic participants. The administrators will find, too, that there are a great many questions in common.

2. *Media Center Institutes*

Several institutes should be established on patterns and schedules that will meet the needs of teachers and aides (as identified by the teachers and aides) in the school or district. Saturday mornings, Wednesday afternoons, summer sessions, and vacation periods should be utilized with provisions for released time, salary credit and stipends, when appropriate.

Courses designed by the *participants* to meet their own recognized needs would be the most beneficial. The consultant or instructor should plan the session *with* the teacher-consumer before they begin.

3. *Experimental or Model Classrooms*

Each school should equip at least one area or instructional space as an experimental or model media learning space. Teaching walls, study carrels, television, teaching desks, audio and video tape equipment, remote control, and dial access systems should be available and used by a teacher trained to *use* the equipment and materials and to *show* others how to use it.

Schedules should then be established to demonstrate lessons, to design new techniques, to bring classes and teachers in for special training, or to evaluate new materials and methods.

4. *Teacher-to-Teacher Seminars*

Teachers in a building, or in many buildings for that matter, need time to work together, to share ideas, to make comparisons, and to create or select needed units, materials and media.

Teacher-to-teacher seminars might be held instead of the many time-consuming and sometimes fruitless faculty meetings in which ignored tasks are often repetitively detailed without action or follow-through. Motivational memos may serve instead of many faculty meetings. Teachers working together to produce what they need to help them with those "slow learners" or that "difficult-to-teach" fractions unit will benefit the instructional process far more than most faculty conferences.

Other exciting projects involving media training that will be described later in the book include a mobile media center, media teaching teams and regional media training centers.

Finally, university courses, industrial training sessions, local in-service programs, and individual tutoring may assist many individuals also. The more ordinary programs often lack the spontaneity, relevance and immediacy of those described above. Indeed, realistic, exciting teacher-training programs that have relevance for today's changing technology, population, and relationships seem to be in order for all areas of education. Preparation of today's youth for tomorrow's world demands the use of contemporary equipment. Indeed, communication itself is, at the very least, dependent on its media.

2

Developing Classrooms
for Maximum Use of
Instructional Media

Planning Learning Environments in New Buildings

When schools are planned, nearly every staff member enthusiastically recommends that classrooms be designed to use media techniques, equipment and materials. Too often, however, the structure that is built often inhibits the use of media. Boxed-in classrooms instead of multimedia learning environments result.

For example, one extremely modern elementary school in the West—designed specifically to facilitate team teaching—has ceilings so low that overhead projectors are almost useless. It would also seem unnecessary and inefficient to troop children all through a building to see a film, when so many structural, administrative and technological alternatives are now available.

Ensure that classrooms are used effectively by considering these guidelines when you are planning new classrooms or a new building:

1. *Light Control.*—If your classrooms feature solid walls of glass, you may have difficulties. Natural light is important, but it can be and should be controlled.

Many states insist that a specified area of each classroom be utilized for windows. Those standards for windows do not usually require "multiwall spread." Window areas may be concentrated in one section of a room, perhaps running from the ceiling to the floor. The rest of the room could contain unobstructed wall area. A high-vision strip around the top of the room is another way to solve the lack of wall space.

In no case, however, should a west wall contain large window areas. Heat buildup and light control may then pose severe problems.

Skylights should not be included in a classroom. They really serve no useful purpose, although some architects and lighting engineers claim they can spread natural light more evenly, especially if coupled with the use of shades. Skylights do make the use of instructional media more difficult, however, and they may lead to major heat problems. They may be attractive in a corridor or reception area, but it is wiser not to plan them for classrooms.

Windows should be equipped with blinds, special opaque shades or heavy drapes. These are readily available from many suppliers, and most are attractive and easy to operate. There is no reason why a classroom cannot have both windows and a media program. Careful planning and "projection" into the situation as it will exist before you build are the only requirements. Further, new screen surfaces, projection systems and transparency colors are overcoming the necessity for darkened classrooms.

2. *Lighting.*—Television, films and filmstrips should not be viewed in total darkness. In addition to possible physical strain, the lack of light makes it difficult, if not impossible, to take notes.

Moreover, total darkness may not be conducive to the proper teaching and learning atmosphere; lack of sleep, interest in coeds, opportunities for mischief, and the absence of visual control may cause problems that would not occur under subdued lighting. In many cases "relevance of curriculum" would seem to increase in direct proportion to the light available as well as the quality of the media presentation. In planning a new school, provide for light-dimming switches in each classroom, as well as for switches that make it possible to turn off the lights in the front or the back of the room without affecting the other lights.

3. *Electrical Outlets.*—Usually there are four or more outlets in a classroom, but invariably they are in the wall baseboards. In most cases this arrangement makes it necessary to run wires from the wall, along the floor, to the place where the projector or other media equipment is being used. It would be wise to plan and place a number of electrical outlets in the floor of your room, approximately in the middle from side to side and at ten-foot intervals, running from the front of the room to the back. Brass plates, placed flush with the floor, are available for covering such outlets.

4. *Sound Projection.*—Many schools have designed and now use operable walls that can be rolled back to transform several classrooms into one large teaching area. They often fail to make provisions for augmenting the volume of the teacher's voice, however.

A teacher who can be heard clearly in a single room may not be audible to the child in the back row of an expanded space. In planning flexible-space classrooms, be certain to include a public address system. Speakers should be placed around the rooms or in the ceiling to provide balanced sound. These additions are relatively inexpensive when planned for the total system and clearly will improve the teaching process.

Other problems may arise in planning projection, multiscreens, and scheduling of students. Careful consideration should be given to all aspects of operable wall utilization before final plans are drawn.

5. *Seeing Is Believing.*—A teacher may stand at the front of her single room and be seen by everybody. When you expand the room she may "shrink" visually and psychologically. If you decide to use large spaces, provide a platform that the teacher can use when she is making presentations. Some schools have found "platform" areas useful in regular classrooms, and, if they are placed in the right position, they may serve both the smaller and larger spaces. If you have platforms in your rooms, don't forget to raise the chalkboards also, or they will be too low to use efficiently. Teachers and students would then have to bend to write, and the vision of students will be partially or totally blocked.

6. *Ceilings.*—Sometimes school districts that are economy-minded expect architects to save money in construction, and, at the same time, they demand the design of better learning spaces. Learning space suffers, however, when ceilings are lowered severely to reduce costs. Do not make ceilings so low that you eliminate the use of overhead projectors and other media equipment.

No ceiling should be lower than ten feet if you wish to use overhead projectors properly. Transparencies should be shown on a tilted screen, and the bottom of the screen will be too low if sufficient ceiling height is not available. If operable walls are to be used to expand several classrooms, a twelve-foot ceiling height is a necessity for any screen in order that children in the back rows may be able to see properly.

Some architects have designed inward-canted walls for the top four feet in elementary schools where ceilings are often only eight or nine feet and usable wall area is eight feet or less. A four-foot "tilt" built into the ceiling design all around the room permits good visibility by any student, no matter where he is sitting, and allows placement of the projector at any convenient place in the room. This flexibility also offers opportunities for differentiated group teaching and team learning, and independent study.

7. *Grouping Classrooms.*—Many of the seemingly odd shapes in class-room construction have been designed to improve instruction through more effective use of media. Rectangular classrooms or "boxes" tend to place some children at a great distance from the front of the room. When two or three rooms are opened by the use of movable walls, the problem becomes enormous. By changing the shapes of the rooms—and grouping them properly—you can greatly reduce the distance between the children and the presentation, once again facilitating good instruction.

One way to build grouped classrooms that have economic as well as educational justification is to begin with a large-group teaching space that can be divided into smaller spaces resulting in better utilization by students through jointly shared media components.

The following selected designs, in this and the next section, were de-veloped by the staff of the Center for Architectural Research (CAR) at Rensselaer Polytechnic Institute, Troy, New York.[1] The first plan, Figure 2-1, provides a large-group divisible space in which media may be used to great advantage in teaching.

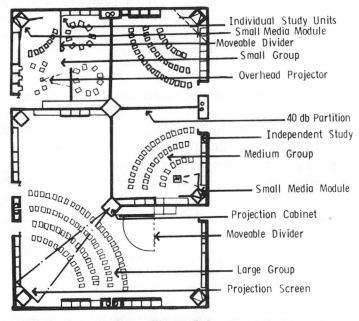

Figure 2-1.

[1] Alan C. Green, M. C. Gassman, *et al; Educational Facilities With New Media, Report B: A Guide for the Design Professions,* The Final Report of an Architectural Research Study Conducted by the Staff of the Center for Architectural Research, School of Archi-tecture, Rensselaer Polytechnic Institute, Troy, New York, Contract No. OE–316–031, U.S. Office of Education, 1966.

The flat floor in the front of the room will seat approximately thirty students in unattached chairs that may be rearranged for small-group, conference, seminar, interview, or other instructional arrangements. The rear sections of the room are located on stepped floors (Figure 2–2), and seating may be on risers with unattached chairs and continuous tables, or floor-mounted tablet-arm chairs. The dividing wall between these rear sections is a permanent one providing necessary acoustical privacy when the rooms are used independently. The folding partitions shown extend halfway across the auditorium and complete the division into three, medium-group rooms.

Media presentations are introduced into the rear sections through front projection of multiple images on a display surface located on the movable partition. The projection equipment is housed in a projection center in the back of the room where it is controlled remotely by the instructor.

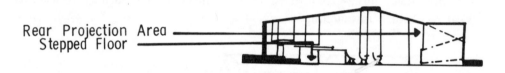

Figure 2–2.

How to Remodel Old Classrooms for Media Teaching

There are occasions when old buildings can be remodeled and used effectively for the newer teaching patterns. When considerations of structure, location, fireproofing, wiring, safety, sanitary facilities, storage, insurance, transportation, and relative total costs are completed, remodeling for media teaching should be considered during deliberations about behavioral objectives, school organization and teacher training. Indeed, the economy of remodeling should probably be weighed during the original "build new vs. refurbish" analysis of an older structure. Further, you may have a structure of considerably less than fifty- or sixty-year-old vintage, yet your newer building may leave much to be desired with respect to media "bouquet" and usability.

In any event, it is relatively easy to change almost any classroom into a media room that is geared to serve large or small groups of students with rear-screen, slide and movie projection, as well as audio tapes and TV. All that is required is a little careful planning.

As indicated earlier, a great deal of planning on this subject was completed by the Center for Architectural Research whose staff has designed a set of practical plans and techniques to enable you to convert classrooms into media rooms.

These plans may be implemented with relative ease and economy and usually without major construction. In fact, it might be possible to use your own district's maintenance personnel. The plans are so practical and easy to implement that any school could probably begin to remodel some classrooms for media instruction within a few weeks, certainly during the summer recess if teachers, consultants, administrators, and maintenance staff are available to plan and work together.

1. Figures 2–3, 2–4 and 2–5 show how a conventional 24- by 32-foot classroom can be altered for multimedia presentations. In what was window space (lower left), a media display center is introduced in the shape of a large cabinet with a screen set into it. This unit contains equipment for rear-screen projection and has chalkboard, corkboard and overhead projection surfaces (see Figure 2–5). This is the focal point for large-group instruction.

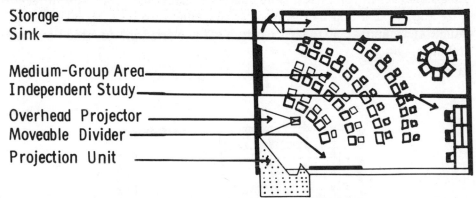

Storage
Sink

Medium-Group Area
Independent Study

Overhead Projector
Moveable Divider

Projection Unit

Figure 2–3.

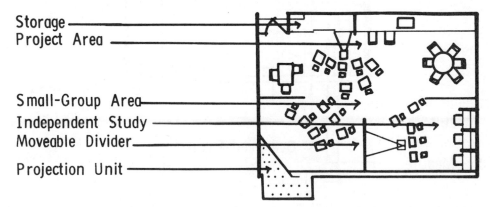

Storage
Project Area

Small-Group Area
Independent Study
Moveable Divider

Projection Unit

Figure 2–4.

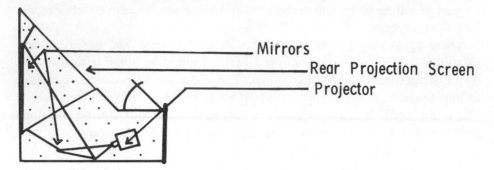

Figure 2–5. New projection devices have reduced the "throw" to less than four feet. (See Teaching Walls, this chapter.)

The room can be quickly converted for small-group instruction when divider panels are swung away from walls to create independent study space (within the dividers) and small-group areas in the rest of the room. The panels also act as corkboard, chalkboard and overhead projection surfaces.

2. Figures 2-6 and 2-7 show how you can convert a typical self-contained elementary classroom to permit wide variations in grouping and activities.

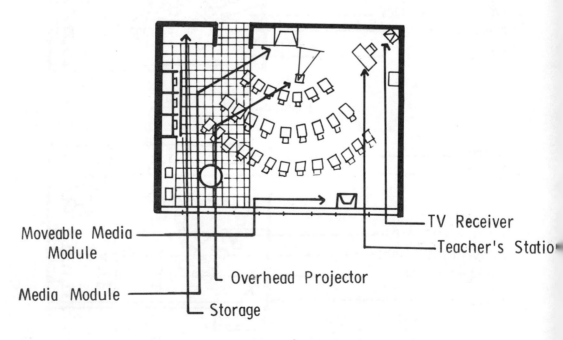

Figure 2–6.

The first plan (Figure 2-6) depicts the room designed for standard class use with students' attention directed to the display surfaces by the seating arrangement. The teacher's station is in the upper right corner below the TV receiver and off to the side of the overhead projection unit. The media module is movable and consists of a rear projection unit and a screen for the overhead projector.

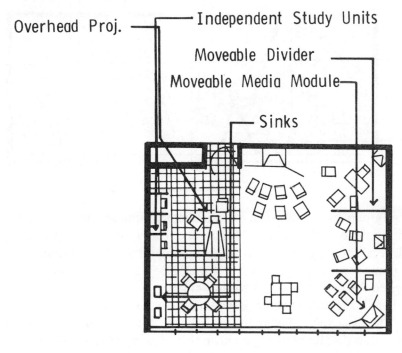

Figure 2–7.

The second plan (Figure 2-7) reveals how the room can be partitioned with movable dividers that also serve as chalkboards and display surfaces. This setup can accommodate small groups working with films, slides and TV; small groups working with the teacher; small groups working on special projects; and individuals working at study carrels. Students may move from group to group and from area to area at any time. The room can easily be shifted back to the basic pattern for presentations to the entire class.

3. Figure 2-8 illustrates how approximately 100 students may be given media instruction in two renovated rooms connected by a media module. This design is particularly appropriate for secondary school use. An instruction area for about thirty students is pictured at the left. Seats occupy about one-third of the two-room unit and are placed so that attention is focused on the TV receivers and the media module that contains slide and overhead projection equipment.

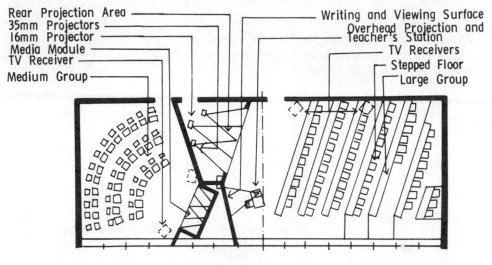

Rear Projection Area ——————
35mm Projectors ——————
16mm Projector ——————
Media Module ——————
TV Receiver ——————
Medium Group ——————

Writing and Viewing Surface
Overhead Projection and
Teacher's Station
TV Receivers
Stepped Floor
Large Group

Figure 2–8.

Large-group instruction can be conducted simultaneously on the other side of the same media module; 35mm and 16mm projectors in the module provide rear projection onto a large screen in the large-group room. A surface for overhead projection (that may also be used for rear projection) is designed for a wall adjacent to the screen.

Seating in the larger room is adequate for approximately seventy students. The seats face diagonally in order to focus attention on rear-projection surfaces while allowing comfortable viewing of overhead projection. The first three rows of seats are on a flat floor and the rest are riser-mounted on a four-step platform. The unattached chairs and writing counters of the first three rows permit the front of this room to be used as a seminar or conference space as well.

4. The simplest and easiest way to remodel a standard classroom is shown in Figure 2–9. Media are again contained in a portable module (lower right) that may be used for 8mm, 16mm or slide projection with a screen surface for overhead projection. The TV receiver is in a mobile cabinet, which also contains recording equipment. Writing and projection surfaces on the other side of the media module complete the installation.

5. Another plan (Figure 2–10) for a media suite of two classrooms joined together requires fairly extensive rebuilding and equipping. Costs are probably as high to complete this kind of remodeling as are those for building two new classrooms. In terms of permitting extensive use of media equipment, however, this could well be the most significant design alteration you could achieve in an existing school building.

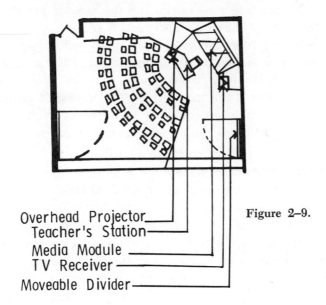

Overhead Projector
Teacher's Station
Media Module
TV Receiver
Moveable Divider

Figure 2–9.

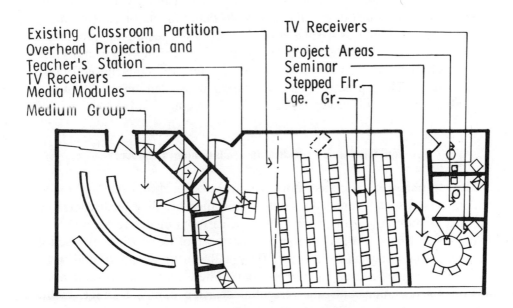

Existing Classroom Partition
Overhead Projection and
Teacher's Station
TV Receivers
Media Modules
Medium Group

TV Receivers
Project Areas
Seminar
Stepped Flr.
Lge. Gr.

Figure 2–10.

The medium-group room (left) seats approximately twenty students, who face a media module (top) from a semicircular seating area. The TV receivers for both rooms are housed in the central module. The lower media module serves the larger room. Facing the module are the room's overhead projector and fifty seats on a stepped floor.

Behind the large-group room are two project areas and a six-person conference room. For these rooms the basic media are TV receivers, 8mm cartridge projectors and overhead projectors.

The various components of this media suite support team teaching, variable grouping patterns, multiclass teaching, independent study, and optimum use of strategically selected and located media equipment.

Professors Green and Gassman point out that the most effective way to introduce media into our educational system is through the renovation of existing classrooms. There are probably over 2,000,000 classrooms requiring remodeling to some extent in more than 120,000 schools and institutions in this country. This consumer market is enormous, and changing any significant percentage of this total for media teaching would do much to improve the effectiveness of instruction and the total educational process.

Conventional classrooms that seat from twenty-five to thirty-five students and that usually range in floor area from 750 to 850 square feet have been the traditional "building blocks" of our "egg-crate" schools for more than 100 years. New buildings being designed and built *today* still feature classroom boxes that flank corridors in time-honored fashion. Citizens, boards of education, administrators, and even state departments of education still cling to the old standards despite enormous strides in technology, industrial techniques, training and learning theory. For this reason Green and Gassman emphasize the need for designing media into the conventional classroom setting. Their practical and functional plans demonstrate that you can remodel your old classroom for media teaching.

Action Guidelines for Building Classroom Resources

Most teachers and administrators are aware of local and regional media centers even if such a center does not exist in their building or district. Few educators ever consider the desirability of classroom media areas, however. These "pocket media centers" may be just the tool to improve instruction with minimum effort and little cost. How will you know where and when to establish a media area in a classroom? These guidelines should assist you on place, timing and other essential decision points. Further, media areas can improve the self-contained classroom as a learning environment and serve to assist the transition to better learning spaces and systems for individual students.

Individualization of Teaching.—Much has been written about the individualization of instruction for students to meet the challenge of individual differences, but relatively little has been printed concerning differences among *teachers* and their instructional styles. Teachers who reach their objectives through student project work, displays and individual effort are to be lauded as much as those who successfully use group dynamics techniques and team learning as their approach. Still others reach learning objectives through experimentation, independent study techniques, team teaching, partnership contracts, even drill reinforcement. Each teacher should have the materials, schedule, assistance, and service he requires to be effective with the students he teaches.

Those teachers who have a facility for using media and materials *require* more of these teaching tools than do their colleagues. They should not be required to stand in line for materials or equipment any more than science teachers who operate active experimental laboratories for all students. Such teachers should be encouraged by administrators to develop their own media corners. Obviously, these should be individualized and not subjected to standardization. These classroom media areas should reflect the particular abilities of each teacher as determined by the needs of his students.

Action Guideline 1: Begin immediately to individualize by ordering and obtaining needed materials, equipment, space, and service in accordance with your developing instructional style. Strong administrative support is required to assist teachers in their professional growth and the improvement of instructional techniques.

Comment: Obtaining Space and Furniture.—Very little is needed to establish media corners for those teachers who are media-oriented. A corner, a table, some chairs, and part of a book shelf may launch an effective media center; at the very least, the seed for a media center will have been planted.

Comment: Obtaining Equipment and Materials.—The money for basic equipment and materials may be obtained from textbook and teaching aid allocations if it is not available as an addition to the budget. Those teachers who wish to establish media corners would undoubtedly exchange part of their workbooks, textbooks, supplies, and other items for the following basic equipment and materials:

Equipment	Utility	Purpose	Approximate Cost
Overhead Projector (for classroom)	Indispensable— can replace some texts and workbooks	For small and large groups; good commercial materials available; individualized materials may be created as well	$100 to $160

Equipment	Utility	Purpose	Approximate Cost
Record Player	Extremely useful	For small and large groups; may be used by individuals and in combination with slides, filmstrips and overhead transparencies	$40 to $60
Filmstrip Previewer	Extremely useful	For individual students; allows them to work at independent study	$20 to $30
Filmstrip Projector	Very useful	For small and large groups; more effective when used in multimedia presentations with a record player and overhead or slide projector	$300 (with sound) $70 to $100 (without sound)
Cassette Tape Recorder	Extremely useful	For individual students, small and large groups; excellent for a wide variety of functions, e.g., instructions to groups, drill, testing, creative independent study, assignments and multimedia teaching	$30 to $130
8mm Film Loop Projector	Very useful	For individuals and small groups; very effective when used with single-concept film loops for individual viewing and reviewing	$100 to $150

Materials

A fairly extensive materials library of single-concept film loops, records, transparencies, and filmstrips is required, of course, but $500 ($1500 would speed the process) per year will soon fill your corner with the materials and instructional equipment you've always wanted. The more expensive items such as the 16mm projector and filmstrip projector with sound may be circulated from the local media center until your budget permits their purchase.

Action Guideline 2: Request additional funds or realign your present allotment to purchase needed media equipment and materials in your next budget request.

Comment: This type of action program to establish classroom media centers is likely to produce interest and motivation in other teachers to utilize media in some aspects of their instructional program. Students will be eager to service and use media corners, and some rooms may become specialized resource areas for language arts, social studies, mathematics, science, art, reading, and other subjects.

Managing Your Own Classroom for Effective Use of Media

An old puzzle that has modern application consists of nine dots in three rows of three. The solution requires that these nine dots be connected by four continuous straight-line segments without removing your pencil from the paper.

Most people "see" the outline of a box and fail to complete the puzzle, i.e.,

or

another version of that "boxed-in feeling."

Indeed, most teachers and administrators are restricted by their egg-crate rooms and buildings. Unfortunately, it is difficult to break out of "boxed-in" schedules, grouping, and teaching. Full schedules and large class loads with little individual or group planning time for teachers and administrators usually keep the entire staff within the framework of the four walls and on a bell schedule. Media can furnish a mighty assistance in any attempt to "break out." * In many instances, it has become the basic ingredient for a true educational "breakthrough"!

At present, instructional techniques designed to answer the needs of individual pupils or small groups are more likely to be found in the ele-

---

* Try this a few times before checking the solution on page 57.

mentary school, while the use of media to serve the academic needs of large groups is more likely to be found in the high school. The extension of the better elementary school instructional methods to the secondary level, and the addition of some of the media practices of the more effective high school instructors to the elementary levels, should be encouraged to meet the needs of all.

Ability or interest groups may utilize a variety of media equipment and materials for different purposes—whether in the high school or in the elementary classroom. For example, a small group of advanced students may be assigned to a section of the room with a tape or record of an outstanding scholar (earphones eliminate noise interference). An overhead projector in another area could provide opportunities for discussion and debate without excessive vocal response. Silent or optical sound loops could be utilized without disturbing other groups. A record and filmstrip presentation might occupy another segment of the class for specific objectives. Students requiring special assistance could utilize previously prepared activity sheets, film loops, filmstrip previewers, or tape recorders. The entire class might be joined at appropriate times to see and hear student or teacher presentations. Finally, a written report or outside research assignment could culminate any or all of these activities.

Naturally, the management situation just described would be enhanced considerably if provision were made to break down the walls of the traditional classroom and library, symbolically at least, by removing schedule and location restrictions. Individual students and groups should be assigned to libraries and other learning spaces. The five 48-minute periods per week at the same time every day in the high school are giving way to modular scheduling, flexible period scheduling and nongraded, "no bell" administrative patterns. These approaches and differentiated teaching assignments, team teaching and small- and large-group instruction are all more effective with the use of good media instruction.

Capitalize on the advantages of these breakthroughs even if these newer organizational and instructional patterns do not exist in your building. First, plan and discuss the new teaching-learning approaches and media usage with the students and other teachers. They are certain to be of assistance in designing more relevant and stimulating lessons. Then bring the design to the principal for approval. There are a number of "learning spaces" in any building, elementary or secondary, for individual and group instruction. These include the library, the science labs, the auditorium, the cafeteria, seminar spaces, conference rooms, guidance quarters, media resource centers, student lounges, or converted storage spaces, if necessary. Finally, the management of the classroom itself may require active assistance from the principal, the central office, custodians, and students to acquire equipment, learning materials and supporting staff as described earlier in this chapter.

One of the best ways to obtain assistance is to seize the initiative by presenting a well-organized plan to the principal, department chairman or supervisor responsible for obtaining equipment (or materials) and teaching aids, and for approving schedules and arranging for other changes. A well-documented proposal that justifies requests should result in full implementation. Inclusion of other teachers in the planning stages is required if they are affected by your suggestions.

As an administrator or supervisor, encouragement and support of plans and requests to improve classroom use for more effective instruction through the use of media are vital—especially if the rooms are designed to meet the learning needs of each student better.

To help build a case (whether you are a teacher, a principal, a supervisor or a superintendent), be certain to obtain all the knowledge and information available on the latest equipment, materials, costs, quality, and effectiveness of the items for the instructional program. The following sources of information and demonstrations are available in the quest to improve teaching and learning through the use of media:

1. *p/i for Schools* is a directory and reference index of almost all materials used in schools, including media materials and equipment. This product magazine is probably circulating in your schools right now. It is sent free of charge to such persons as media directors, librarians and school principals.

2. Almost every manufacturer of media materials and equipment publishes a listing or catalog of his entire school product line. Many will give free demonstrations to describe the "superiority" of their product.

3. There are many publications that list a variety of media equipment and materials representative of the industry. For example, the National Audio Visual Association (NAVA) publishes an equipment directory; Educators Progress Service, Randolph, Wisconsin, publishes several annotated directories of free or inexpensive materials, sample titles of which are *Educators Guide to Free Films, Educators Guide to Free and Inexpensive Materials;* NICEM (National Information Center for Educational Media) provides annotated film lists for personalized cataloging; *Bertha Landers Reports* supplies current film reviews as does EFLA (Educational Film Library Association) in card form; the Library of Congress will furnish cards for non-print as well as print materials; *Audio Cardalog* publishes annotated reviews in card form for new audio productions.

4. There are several magazines devoted exclusively to media, such as *Audiovisual Instruction,* featuring media utilization and equipment evalua-

tion; *AV Guide,* a similar magazine; and *AV Communication Review,* a research-oriented media publication.

5. Finally, refer to the list of selected readings at the end of this book for in-depth media information.

Using Media Equipment Extensively and Effectively

The amount of money spent in the median school district for media equipment, materials and salaries increased from less than two dollars per elementary pupil in 1962–1963 to five dollars per pupil in 1970–1971.[2] It is anticipated that the four-dollar figure will hold or increase in the years ahead. Districts are expending more and more money on the "newer" media items, such as video tapes, video recorders, and TV cameras, according to *School Management.*[3]

There is no guarantee, however, that this equipment is being used as well or as extensively as it should be used by classroom teachers. In fact, there is ample evidence to indicate that it is not. In too many districts sizable media collections are simply standing idle too much of the time.

There are a number of ways to encourage greater teacher use of the new teaching media. Perhaps the most effective way is by remodeling one or two classrooms in a district—or in every school in the district—into special media "showcases."

The idea is not to create a seldom-used museum of hardware and materials. These remodeled classrooms may be used by regular teachers and classes to perform a demonstration function for other teachers; or they may be used periodically by every teacher. In either case, the special media areas may serve as effective vehicles for creating staff demand for the new media.

More conventional means of supervising the use of media usually involve a building coordinator. The media specialist for a building (or audiovisual coordinator as he is still known in many schools) often does not have the time, professional background or experience to assist teachers in the tasks they view as most important.

Eleanor Godfrey gathered evidence which revealed this educational dilemma through a survey that involved 517 schools from 247 school districts with enrollments of from 150 to 25,000, from all parts of the country including urban, suburban and rural areas. In summarizing the charts and observations of the report in the DAVI Monograph on "The State of Audio-

---

[2] "The Cost of Audio-Visual Instruction, 1970–71," *School Management* (October, 1970), p. 26.

[3] *Ibid.,* p. 29.

visual Technology: 1961–1966," [4] some disturbing conclusions may be drawn with respect to supervising the use of media:

1. Few school districts outside of large metropolitan or suburban systems have *full-time* media directors.

2. The percentage of districts with no media director and those that utilize the principal, assistant principal or classroom teacher is overwhelming when measured against those that do employ media coordinators, librarians and district level personnel.

	None, Principal or Teacher	Coordinator or Librarian
Elementary	81%	19%
High School	77%	23%

3. These figures are especially significant when analyzed with the "Characteristics of Audiovisual Coordinators." Only thirty-four per cent of the elementary and twenty-six per cent of the secondary coordinators had college plus in-service training. Eighty-seven per cent of the elementary and seventy-five per cent of the secondary coordinators spent one quarter or less of their time on media duties. For the most part coordinators apparently function chiefly as logistics specialists who order and schedule equipment and materials.

4. There are wide discrepancies between the coordinator's tasks and the kinds of assistance that teachers desire. Teachers want help in keeping up to date on new media materials (rank order one) and suggestions for appropriate materials (rank order two). Tasks performed by coordinators and desired by principals include the ordering and scheduling of media (rank order one) and the teaching of equipment operation (rank order two).

In addition to providing a media "showcase" or demonstration room for each building, the preceding survey would seem to suggest four major recommendations for the more effective utilization of media.

Recommendations:

1. Employ full-time media specialists for building coordination.

2. Relieve coordinators (and teachers) of clerical, maintenance and custodial chores.

3. Increase the training, experience and performance requirements for professional media specialist certification and qualification.

---

[4] Eleanor P. Godfrey, *The State of Audiovisual Technology: 1961–1966,* Monograph No. 3 (Washington, D.C.: Department of Audiovisual Instruction, National Education Association, 1967), p. 46. (Material is based on a series of four studies conducted by The Bureau of Social Science Research, Inc., pursuant to contracts with the U.S. Office of Education under the provisions of NDEA Title VII.)

4. Develop teacher-media coordinator workshops and in-service courses to increase the agreement between them on the service functions of media specialists. (Certainly the primary goal of these sessions should be the improvement of instruction.)

Two Innovative Plans: The Teaching Desk and the Teaching Wall

Recently, "innovation" has been distinguished from "invention." Invention in education, as in industry or science, might be deemed a device or procedure *conceived or made by original effort."* An innovation might be described as a device or method *newly introduced* in your district, school or classroom. This distinction might be considered educational hairsplitting, but it is indicated here to emphasize the value of *application* in education. It would be difficult (and unnecessary) to ascribe media "inventions" to procedures or devices that many could claim as their own original creations. The important thing is *to innovate* for improvement, for solving a difficult problem or for overcoming existing obstacles. To innovate is to use inventions or new ideas in your existing classroom situation. The examples of inventions described below (if they are inventions) would certainly be innovations in many classrooms, if the objective is to develop maximum use of instructional media.

A Multimedia Teacher's Desk.—One inventor-innovator, Dr. Paul I. McClendon of Oral Roberts University, responded to the need of creative teachers to use every available medium of instruction suited to meet their teaching objectives by designing an integrated multimedia teacher's desk.

The problem, of course, was the average classroom with its unwieldly and non-functional desk, lack of screen and proper electrical facilities, the carts, tables, extension cords, projection screens, and reliance on delivery from an outside source. The "inventor's" solution (the teaching desk) concentrates all of the stimuli near the teacher *and* is controlled by him, thus greatly improving the total instructional climate.

Dr. McClendon designed the teacher's console to be equipped with a self-storing folding lectern, an overhead transparency projector, a 2×2 slide projector, and an audio tape recorder. The design pattern is well integrated to permit maximum flexibility in using all media components within the teacher's desk and those that are external to it.

The overhead transparency projector is conveniently located on the right side of the media desk mounted to the top surface. Since the projection stage is at desk height, the teacher need not flex his arm nor make other distracting motions at chest height, as is often the case when overhead projectors are wheeled in. Only a slight tilt of the projection bed is necessary to permit projection onto an angled screen above the chalkboard behind the teacher.

On the left side of the media desk two hinged doors in the top open to a compartment containing the 2 × 2 slide projector and an audio tape recorder-player. The slide projector is mounted at an angle to project without keystoning. A full remote-control cord can be drawn out for the teacher's use in the event he may wish to move around or use a pointer during the slide projection. An auxiliary classroom light switch is immediately adjacent to turn room lights off when necessary to add brilliance to the projected slides.

The self-storing lectern is one of the most useful features. The lectern folds down for storage, making a flat desk top. When raised for use, it locks in place. The tape recorder microphone plugs into a receptacle on the raised lectern for use while the teacher is standing. Another receptacle mounted on the opened surface of the compartment door provides proper microphone placement for the seated teacher and also serves as the microphone storage retainer when the compartment is locked.

The projection screen is matte finished and fixed-mounted in an open position above head level over the chalkboards. This arrangement eliminates the awkward disadvantage of the teacher having to raise and lower or set up and take down the screen—perhaps during the class period—often covering up other display areas. It is also more convenient for students who have only to raise their eyes slightly above the teacher's head rather than to completely divert their attention to another part of the room. Simultaneous use of the overhead and slide projectors is possible with each using half of the projection screen width or by installing two matte-projection screens above the chalkboards.

Possibly the greatest advantage of the multimedia desk is that it is a self-contained, permanently installed, integral part of the teacher's total instructional complex. The multimedia desk is always there. The teacher knows that at any given moment all of these facilities will be available to him at the flick of a switch. Convenience, flexibility and function are happily integrated in one unit. Dr. McClendon has certainly taken steps actively to create and implement a better classroom media program.[5]

A Multimedia Teaching Wall.—Another innovator, U.S. Army Education Specialist John H. Krickel, made an old room over for full media

---

[5] The integrated media desk instructional system was designed by Paul I. McClendon, "Oral Roberts University's Dial Access Audio-Video System," *Audiovisual Instruction* (May, 1967), pp. 464–466. A complete set of construction drawings, lens, design, and equipment data for the multimedia desk is available to educators by request from Dr. McClendon, 7878 South Oswego, Tulsa, Oklahoma 74135.

utilization by designing a multimedia teaching wall. He implemented the project by employing the school custodial staff, some lumber, a great deal of ingenuity, and very little money. He developed a method for installing a full rear-screen projection system—without tearing down walls or redesigning circuits.

Rear-screen projection is receiving wider acceptance as a media technique that offers great advantages to schools. It removes projectors from the classrooms and places the teacher in front of the class where he can work *with* the film or filmstrip—not *at* the projector. Further, the student sees an image that "comes right out of the screen." Although the advantages of rear projection have been known for some time, few schools have adopted it because of what seemed to be prohibitive remodeling costs. Krickel's design removes the excessive cost barrier.

Made of prefinished plywood panels that are within the reach of any district's budget, the teaching wall is placed *between the class and the old front wall*. It partitions off just six or seven feet of floor space. Rear-projection screens are mounted in the wall and are covered by sliding chalkboards. When a teacher wishes to, he slides the boards away and shows either filmstrips or a sound film.

Behind the teaching wall, made of mill-dressed two-by-four lumber, is a large bookcase. The top shelf is about eight feet high. The projectors stand on this shelf and are aimed at mirrors. A slide projector and a filmstrip projector can also be mounted on the shelf and aimed at a second mirror, to be reflected to a second screen.

The key to the system is the control lectern Krickel has devised. This device is situated at the front of the room between the two screens. The teacher can use switches and relays to dim lights, start projectors, or shift from slide to movie. A recent estimation reveals that a teacher giving a media presentation spends ten to fifteen per cent of the class period in walking to the light switches, walking back to the projector, walking from the projector to the screen to point at a picture, etc.

Here, the media control board does all the work. Such a board—in heavy-duty, unglamourized form—costs a few dollars for switches and can be assembled very quickly.

The teacher simply places selected filmstrip cartridges and a roll of film into the projectors in the partitioned room. He spends between ninety seconds and two minutes on the task.

The most expensive apparatus (besides the projectors) are the screens. Plastic membrane rear-projection screens (72 × 48 inches) cost approximately $50 to $75.

Newer refinements to Krickel's teaching wall (which involved the use of mirrors to reflect projected images onto the rear plastic screens) include mirrors *integrated with the lenses* of motion picture and carousel slide projectors. The projectors are then mounted *parallel* to the screens and reduce needed space behind the teaching wall to less than four feet! [6]

It probably is possible to place the teaching console or desk on wheels and move it to different teaching stations if your district cannot afford to build them in quantity at first. Similarly, the teaching wall could be designed in four-by-seven or eight-foot portable sections and erected in scheduled rooms or areas, if this proves more feasible in any given situation.

In any event, the total cost to install a teaching desk and a teaching wall need not exceed $200 and $1000 respectively—a small investment that can bring rather substantial returns in the form of teaching-learning excitement for teachers and students alike.

Solution to puzzle that appears on page 49:

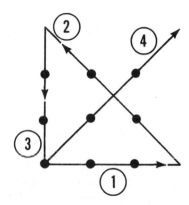

---

[6] Jack Tanzman, "How to Remodel A Classroom for AV Teaching," *School Management* (September, 1965), pp. 122, 124.

3

Establishing the Media
Center as a Resource
for Better Instruction

Designing a Media Resource Center for an Existing Building

Many educators think of a media center as a million-dollar complex that houses a tremendous inventory of equipment and supplies, a sizable staff of technicians, facilities for programing materials into classrooms, and experienced teachers who demonstrate sophisticated techniques. This is a utopian concept.

Realistically, this type of resource center may exist to serve an entire district or region. Even where a district or regional center exists, however, every teacher must have *immediate* access to certain instructional materials. There should be a simple media center in every school; one that enables staff members to obtain films, tapes, records, maps, and transparencies *when* they are needed. Indeed, this should be a minimum requirement for an instructional program.

To bring the concept of a media resource center into the realm of the immediately obtainable, nothing more is required than a place to keep *noncirculating* materials that teachers use in the classroom. It can be part of the library, a remodeled office or a renovated area in the basement. The objective is to locate suitable media space in a school, find a relatively inexpensive way to fill it with practical, useful items, and design a system to make it easy for teachers to use those items effectively—and often.

Any school can create its own simple media center without spending a great deal of money simply by making creative use of what it already has. Before this is done, however, teachers (or administrators) must be convinced that they need one. Demonstrations should clarify how media can make their jobs easier and more interesting. The space for a media resource center can be found more easily when school people really want one!

The needed space was found in East Memorial Elementary School in Farmingdale, New York, when three guidance counselors were moved out of a three-room complex and stationed in different parts of the building in order to become more accessible to the students.

The partitions were removed in the 400-square-foot area that had served as their offices, and the area was then redivided into spaces for housing, preparing and learning how to use materials. In contrast to this example, other schools have redesigned libraries, corridors and unused classrooms.

Strategies for Managing an Effective Media Center

One approach for stretching the use of media materials, as we have already suggested, would include locating all available items in a center, assigning responsibility to a single professional and providing technical and clerical assistance as well as training for that individual.

Suppose this idea is not appealing. Perhaps the potential hazards seem greater than the possible rewards. In any event, a return to the old notion of storing media equipment and materials in the principal's office usually results in non-use of media resources. Media materials and equipment should be used, and used effectively.

Here is one technique that may insure the appropriate use of materials. Establish *a media corner* in the library of each school—a place where equipment and materials may be seen, used and demonstrated. (Where there is no library, the same idea may be implemented in a classroom, in unused or renovated space or, if necessary, in the reception area.)

The advantages of establishing such a media corner are threefold.

First, the equipment is no longer stored somewhere—it is on display. Marketing people discovered long ago that supermarket displays are much more enticing than the under-counter storage of the corner grocery stores.

Second, because equipment is on display where teachers meet, it is discussed. Teachers see overhead projectors or slide projectors and talk about presentations they have made with them—*and they learn and assist each other.*

Photo 7. Portable record players, tape recorders, projectors, books, and viewers may be used by students in media corners established by teachers and librarians. (Photograph courtesy of Amo DeBernardis, President, Portland Community College, Portland, Oregon.)

Third, the corner permits the media specialist, the librarian, or an interested teacher, to develop media displays that may further encourage the use of these tools. Displays may range from an outstanding group presentation, to the work of an individual teacher, to the exhibit of new materials and supplies.

Another technique that may help draw teachers' attention to available media equipment and materials would be the distribution of frequent "bulletins" detailing all the films, filmstrips, projectuals, etc., currently owned by the school—including suggested uses—supplemented by monthly bulletins of new acquisitions. Neither of these are difficult to continue once the first compilation has been made, and they may be kept current by any clerk who is informed as new materials are purchased. The bulletin may take the form of an advertisement, a newspaper or a telegram. Students and faculty could assist, and bulletin boards or displays would speed information on what is available to all staff members.

Sometimes planned and focused communication is effective in establishing awareness of the need for a school-based media center that the teachers *want* to use. One principal's method for getting teachers to start using media presentations involves bringing to their attention specific items that they may use for particular presentations.

This "media specialist" reviews each teacher's projected unit plans at the beginning of the year and selects areas that he thinks lend themselves to effective media teaching with materials that the school owns. When teachers request equipment and select materials, he then circulates a bulletin that indicates that "Miss Jones" will be using the overhead projector on a particular day to make a presentation on arithmetic, "Miss Smith" will be using the filmstrip projector and "Miss Thompson" will be using the motion picture projector in order to teach specific concepts, skills or content. "After a few weeks of this," he reports, "a media awareness begins to be built up in the school."

Sometimes, of course, the building administrator becomes so involved in everyday "line" problems—irate parents with individual complaints, a flood in the basement, late buses—that he may overlook the potential value of media for improving instruction. Indeed, he may even become so immersed in daily problems that he temporarily forgets the major purposes of his school. In this event the experienced *teacher* must serve as the catalyst to bring innovation in media instruction to the school by setting an example, starting a pilot or encouraging the principal to visit a good media resource center as a possible model for his building. In fact, some teachers' groups are now seeking to obtain agreements from school boards that provide for the inclusion of media centers, classrooms, staff, and equipment in the school budget.

A Checklist and Standards for Developing a Local Center: Content, Equipment and Staff

This checklist was developed by the authors from lists supplied by school districts (with adequate to superior media programs), NEA-DAVI "starter sets," state departments of education, media directors, and supervisors. It is also based on current instructional trends. This list is not as ambitious as the one published by the American Association of School Librarians and the Department of Audiovisual Instruction of the National Education Association's *Standards for School Media Programs*,[1] which represents ultimate goals. Rather, the checklist represents goals realistically obtainable in a relatively short period of time.

Naturally, the standards recommended here are subject to a number of variables including curriculum decisions, types of students, priorities, loca-

---

[1] American Association of School Librarians, *Standards for School Media Programs* (Washington, D.C.: Department of Audiovisual Instruction, National Education Association, 1969).

tion of school, grade range, organization of district, training and background of teachers, and rapid changes in technology and society itself. On balance, however, the proposed checklist might be considered as a good set of "conscience standards" or *minimum foundations* for schools that are not now making the most of visual stimuli for the purpose of improving teaching and learning.

The list is proposed for current elementary school buildings with enrollments of 500 students. Upward adjustments should be made for secondary schools. One yardstick that might be applied would be to increase the following items by substituting 250 students to be served by the recommended amounts for middle schools and junior high schools and 200 students for high schools. Remember, these recommendations are *basic* and do not include special multimedia needs for a nongraded organization, team teaching and individualized instruction.

Content

Perhaps the easiest task in beginning a local media center is stocking the center with books and teaching materials. These probably already exist in classrooms, storage areas, the principal's office, teachers' room, and on the tops of student clothes closets. A staff committee assisted by a school secretary and clerk could gather and inventory what is available in a relatively short time. A media specialist or librarian (full- or part-time) could aid the staff in relating what exists to the curriculum and in cataloging it for easy accessibility and effective use. The task of filling gaps becomes easier when it can be seen on charts that list exactly what the gaps are!

Materials and Instructional Aids	Recommendation (No. of Titles)	Comments	Your School's Inventory
Filmstrips	1000	Cataloged, cross-indexed and placed on heavy-duty wall racks	
Phonograph records and tape recordings	1000	Cataloged, cross-indexed, annotated for effective use, and stored for easy accessibility	
Field trip file	yes!	Annotated, cross-indexed with evaluation comments	
35mm slides	1000	Cataloged and programed for use with phonograph records and/or audio tapes	

Materials and Instructional Aids	Recommendation (No. of Titles)	Comments	Your School's Inventory
8mm films	500	"Single-concept," cataloged and indexed for easy reference	
16mm films	0–100	Several thousand film titles should be available to teachers on a daily delivery basis from a central film library. Some films should be available in the building, depending on effective use, the students and the curriculum	
Overhead transparencies	2000	Cataloged with teachers' guides and background material	
Maps and globes	50	Cataloged for use with curriculum guides	
Photographs, prints, teaching boards, etc.	1000	Cataloged, cross-indexed and kept in good repair with file cards of teaching ideas, stimulating questions and suggestions	
Bulletin board file	100	Exemplary photographs, prints, samples of outstanding bulletin board items and ideas	
Multimedia kits	50	Packaged materials selected from the above for use with a specific subject area or on a particular grade level	
Books [2]	10,000	Cataloged, stored and easily accessible; with cross-indexed file cards and annotations to encourage use with individual students and groups. Union cataloged with all other media where applicable	
Magazines	50		
Newspapers, pamphlets and clippings	5		

[2] In this book media refers to all forms of communication.

Materials and Instructional Aids	Recommendation (No. of Titles)	Comments	Your School's Inventory
Professional materials for the faculty		Curriculum guides and materials, teachers' guides and manuals, annotations, composites and compilations of research topics and writings on such areas as team teaching, slow learners and individual instruction are extremely useful	
Books	1000		
Magazines	50		

All items should be selected by a trained team with continuing evaluation performed on the basis of carefully developed criteria. The team approach is discussed in chapter 4.

There is nothing astonishing about the list. It includes standard and new teaching items that every school should have. The major purpose of a media center, however, is to centralize a school's arsenal of media materials and equipment for easy accessibility. (Too often media items are scattered over a district or region and no one really knows where they all are.)

For instructional technology to be efficient, and useful, everyone should know where everything is, what is available and how to obtain what is needed. In addition, if the center is properly staffed with trained personnel who know how to serve teachers, everyone will learn how to use it effectively.

Equipment

Production equipment and the proper use of supplies require trained personnel. Specialists (teachers or aides with art and technical skills) should work with the staff for the purpose of improving teaching and learning. Slides and materials produced by amateur photographers on the staff, in the community or from the student body may be extremely effective and should be used when appropriate. Indeed, student and teacher involvement in creating the "stuff of learning" can prove to be exciting and rewarding. This last comment will be described more completely in chapters 7 and 8.

One or more teachers in the building with semi-professional ability (or a photographer employed by the district on a part-time basis) should be utilized for producing transparencies, prints, enlargements, murals, study boards, offset reproductions, activity sheets, and other instructional materials. Part-time graphics and technical assistants or aides are essential in the absence of trained staff members. Eventually, a full-time media staff should be employed. Above all do not be discouraged if there is a lack of trained personnel. Begin with what you have—teachers, administrators and secretaries with ability, creativity, and desire to do a better job with students. The suggestions on continuing education offered in chapters 1 and 4, and in larger centers described at the end of this chapter, will be easier to plan and implement once the local media center is established.

Training may be obtained from universities, adult education courses and "how-to" kits and books. Technicians and aides may be employed on a part-time basis, and volunteers may be found in the community and within the student body. The planning needed, and even the trial and error, will be part of the pleasure and pain of the process of beginning something that will improve the instruction of students. The important thing to remember about beginning a media center (or anything worthwhile) is *to begin*. The following equipment recommendations are more than a beginning but do represent a most realistic approach to quality education:

Type	Recommendation	Comments	Your School's Inventory
Production equipment			
* View or press camera	1	The equipment should include assorted lenses, e.g., wide-angle, close-up, light meters and basic film types plus high speed film	
Rapid process camera	1		
2 × 2 slide camera	1		
8mm motion picture camera	1	The equipment should include zoom attachments, exposure attachment, tripod, viewer, editing splicer, etc.	
* Dark room	1	There should be basic equipment and supplies: photocopying equipment, copy stand, lights, etc.	
* Offset press (small)	1	A trained operator may be required for producing instructional materials as well as for printing clear and legible tests, administrative memoranda, forms, and curriculum guides. This outfit should include a full complement of equipment and supplies,	

Type	Recommen-dation	Comments	Your School's Inventory
		e.g., inks, mattes, offset bond, fountain concentrate, desensitizer, etc. It may be necessary to share this equipment with other schools for efficient use	
Picture-mounting equipment	1 complete set	Specialists or aides should be available to assist teachers in this area. This set should include a full complement of equipment and supplies, e.g., dry mount press, hand iron, weights, heavy cardboard, laminating film and machine, razor blades, X-acto knives, trimmers, rubber cement, mounting tissue, etc.	
Graphics equipment	1 complete set	A specialist or aide should be available to assist teachers in this area. This set should include a full complement of equipment and supplies, e.g., dry transfer letters, masking tape, felt pens, drawing boards, rubber cement, construction paper, primary boldface typewriter, stencil guides, T-squares, triangles, French curves, felt and flannel boards, etc.	
Transparency-making equipment		A specialist or aide should be available to assist teachers in this area.	
Heat process machine	2		
Diazo process machine	1		
* Photocopy machine	1		

* Highly desirable—not required to begin.

The preparation or production area in a small media center need not be a highly technical complex. It should be a place where teachers can prepare instructional materials for their classrooms quickly and economically with the aid of a graphics specialist.

There should be facilities for producing filmstrips so that a teacher returning from a trip may use her own slide pictures for the production of a filmstrip for the whole staff.

Teachers' slides, and slides from other sources, may be duplicated to build a backlog for classroom use. Teachers, or whoever takes the pictures, can prepare scripts for sound tapes to play with the slides. In this way sequential units may be developed and programed for use in simple slide projectors of the "carousel" type.

Staff

The latest standards for staffing media centers [3] recommend one full-time media specialist for every 250 students. According to these guidelines, an optimum situation in an elementary school might include a professionally certified and qualified "head of the media center," an assistant, a graphics technician, a photographic technician, and a clerk-typist for a 500-pupil elementary school. Complicating the problem at this stage of media evolution are the situations where libraries exist apart from "audio-visual" programs. If we add librarians and clerks to the list above, an elementary school might be expected to employ as many as eight full-time staff members for its needed media functions.

How can a school begin, when it does not have the financial resources to staff a media center on the scale described above?

After finding the space and cataloging what exists in the building (perhaps by using student or faculty teams during paid summer employment), the school should enlist its own faculty as specialists until additional staff can be employed. Indeed, it may be a great deal easier to convince central office administrators, the board of education and the community of your need when a faculty demonstrates what it can do with limited staff and facilities and then recommends an improved situation. Only a small minority is likely to say "keep up the good work." Support will come from the majority who appreciate effort, ingenuity and planning to improve the instruction of students.

If a school is partially or completely departmentalized, subject specialist teachers may be programed for service in the center for perhaps forty minutes each day. Rather than supervising the cafeteria during their open periods, these teachers will be performing educationally meaningful jobs. Each teacher should be responsible for a specific aspect of the center.

[3] American Association of School Librarians, *Standards for School Media Programs.*

Schools without departmentalization may establish similar procedures through coverage during lunch and bus duty periods, release time during gym and music classes, and by being freed of clerical chores. Relatively little money would be needed to employ part-time clerks and aides for this purpose.

One teacher could become a specialist in filmstrips. She must know what is available and develop frequency-of-use charts. This instructor could learn how to make filmstrips and control purchasing to avoid repetition. She could also instruct teachers in the instructional use of filmstrips and, possibly, in their preparation and production.

Other teachers may concentrate on different aspects or functions of the center and on becoming familiar with all the materials available in their own subject matter specialty. In this way the school will develop resource experts without being forced to employ additional staff, and a beginning could be made.

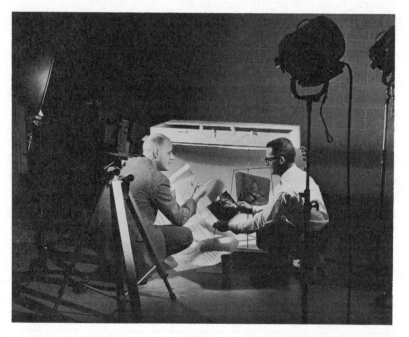

Photo 8. The art director and the photographer discuss a layout before shooting. At one end of this large room used for photographic setups is a rack containing large rolls of colored paper used for backdrops. (United States Air Force Academy Photo.)

What about a technician to operate the more sophisticated equipment and solve special production problems? One of the teachers with an art background could work with transparencies and other media materials. He might become the "technician." If possible, part-time or consultant technicians in graphics and photography could be employed or assigned from a regional center for one day a week.

While a relatively small percentage of the staff frequently forms the nucleus of the center's manpower, the *majority* of the teachers should work in the center. Monthly and summer workshops, conducted in the conference area of the center, would insure effective use of the center.

This, then, is a fundamental "teachers' media resource center." It is not overly sophisticated or complicated. It is neither big, ultramodern nor imposing. It is not expensive. But it can be a useful, practical facility for helping teachers and administrators to help themselves to do a more effective instructional job.

Guidelines for Staffing a Center with Specialists

At what point do you need a specialist in your school's media center? Who should he be, and what should he do? There are no easy answers to these questions, but a few generalizations may be cited.

First, and foremost, you have no media program unless someone is specifically charged with running it. This person may be a full- or part-time employee at the start—a teacher, librarian or principal (but not a clerk). Eventually the teacher may become the media specialist needed to operate a top-flight media center.

Second, the responsibility of the person in charge of the media program is *not* that of keeping track of films and filmstrips, nor is it repairing projectors and other equipment. These tasks should be performed by a clerk—preferably one assigned to work for the media program coordinator.

Third, the responsibility of the person in charge of the program should be to *help plan* effective instructional programs and improved curricula. He may not be an expert technician or repairman, but he must be an excellent teacher—one who can innovate instructional techniques or assist others in the development of teaching concepts through media materials and methods.

In an elementary school a highly skilled principal might serve (temporarily) as the media program coordinator. This function might also be assigned to an assistant principal or to a librarian, if he or she is truly equipped to handle the role and has the time and interest. Otherwise, the best possible arrangement would be to designate a creative and knowledgeable classroom teacher to spend half of his or her time as the building media coordinator with no class assignments during that portion of the day.

In a junior or senior high school of any size, the staff should include at least one person who is directly in charge of media activities. Ideally, a high school might have an assistant principal in charge of the instructional program, which could well emanate from the media resource center. He should be supported by noncertified staff—a clerk, a graphics specialist and a technician. If separate space or staff are not immediately available for a media center, a portion of the library and its staff might serve to begin a program.

Since the techniques of graphics have training potential, the person in charge of this segment of the program might be the graphic arts teacher specifically retained for the role. He might be located in the media resource center and he could train students through a work-experience program, which may be superior to the usual industrial graphics arts course.

If this concept is considered, you may find that in high schools of any size the personnel needed are already on the staff. All that is required is to realign some of their present responsibilities. But remember, this is only a description of *how to get started*. A combination library-media resource center should eventually be phased into a carefully designed and planned media center with qualified personnel and training facilities.

Creating a Districtwide Center on a Limited Budget

A media center need *not* cost a million dollars, particularly if some of those old, unused spaces that may be wasting away on school properties are reexamined.

In Montgomery County, Maryland, for example, schoolmen transformed an old gymnasium (left standing when a school burned down) into a badly needed—and very modern—districtwide media center. Total renovation costs were less than $10,000.

The gymnasium had been scheduled to be torn down. Instead, it has become the means for consolidating the district's entire media operation. Probably every district in the country has a building, or part of a building, going to waste. If not, there must be a suitable house, store front or building available in the district. This type of search could well provide the impetus for the beginning of a district media center.

The deserted building originally had been remodeled to house administrative offices. Air conditioning was already in use, the main floor ceiling had been lowered (to cut heating costs) and adequate lighting had been installed. Only a minimum amount of remodeling was needed to outfit the facility as a media center—and the district's own maintenance staff completed this task.

For its modest investment, the district was able to establish (on one floor) a materials and library services center and a large central lecture-demonstration area where teachers are shown how to use media materials and equipment. By completely enclosing a small corner area and installing some old sinks, a darkroom was created. Another large area was converted for storage. In the central area, office-work spaces for the technicians were designed to service all efficiently.

On the floor below (formerly locker rooms) a processing and inventory center was established. Here the schools in the district are serviced through order processing, cataloging, numbering, etc. Almost no major work was required for this vital area; only movable shelving, equipment and a few partitions had to be installed.

Now the former gymnasium functions smoothly as the media production and processing center for every school in the huge Montgomery County district; a fleet of delivery-and-order trucks is in constant motion.

Developing the Ideal Media Center: Some Important Principles

If a "million dollars" are available, and a school administration will support it, you may build a facility very much like the media resource center in Cooke Library at the Punahou School in Honolulu, Hawaii. This may be one of the best instructional media centers currently in operation.

The way it is constructed—and used—emphasizes some obvious but important principles in media center planning and operation; principles that apply, whatever the cost of the center.

For example, the media center should be designed specifically to serve the students and the teachers. Too many centers are simply noninstructional additions to existing library facilities, built to stockpile media equipment. The Punahou School center—although it houses the school's books as well as media equipment and supplies—is designed to support the curriculum.

Its facilities include motion pictures, slide films, microfilms, recordings, teaching machines, and audio and video taped lessons—all of them chosen and produced *expressly* to complement the school program.

Services of this center are not limited to the facility itself. An overhead projector and a ceiling-mounted tilt-screen have been installed in every one of the school's 136 instructional areas, and a remote-control phrase-repeating device permits the use of thirty taped programs at individual language study stations.

Second, the media center needs to be large enough. Size depends on the *use* of the center, of course. If it is designed only to store machinery and software, the center may be limited in size—and will probably be just as limited in educational effectiveness.

The ideal center will provide appropriate independent study space for every student and will include ample facilities for materials preparation and teacher training.

The Punahou School's instructional materials center meets this second principle perfectly. Covering almost three-quarters of an acre, its two levels comprise 36,000 square feet—more than twenty square feet per child. In addition to ample storage space for books and other instructional materials, the building has been planned to include study carrel areas, study halls, conference rooms, special subject work areas, art studios, and faculty work areas, as well as space for media equipment and a preparation room for making new instructional materials.

Then, too, the ideal media center should be staffed by persons with an understanding of the multiple-resource approach to education and a sensitivity to teachers' problems and needs.

The heart of Punahou's media center is its staff—a dedicated group of media specialists and trained librarians. The media department is under the direction of a former teacher whose special competence is graphics production.

The center's instructional materials preparation room includes facilities for making overhead transparencies, 35mm slides, graphs, charts, posters, dry mounts, color lifts, laminations, duplicate and facsimile reproductions, black and white (and color) study or display prints, filmstrips, 16mm motion pictures, enlargements or reductions from books or magazines, duplicate slides, and other special materials.

To insure that these facilities are used effectively and are of service to teachers, the center's director spends one quarter of his time making regular visits to every classroom in the school. These are followed with individual teacher conferences and meetings with entire departments to discuss the use of media to solve teaching problems.

A media curriculum committee works with the director to establish broad policies for operation and use of the center's media and facilities. Special in-service programs are available to all teachers.

The ideal instructional materials center should, of course, be accessible to all, easily used and pleasant in atmosphere; all materials in the center— not just books—should circulate.

In Punahou's fan-shaped center, all materials—including media programs—are arranged for easy access. The librarian, or media secretary, does *not* stand between the library user and the materials and equipment. Check-out procedures are simple and completed easily and quickly. Individual study carrels provide space and adequate power to run the library's media equipment.

More than this, students are encouraged to participate in running the center. More than fifty of them are scheduled to join in the production and processing of the center's instructional materials. Many have reached near-professional sophistication in handling the equipment.

Finally, the ideal media center should be open for use before and after the academic class day as well as from 9:00 A.M. to 3:00 P.M. This may seem self-evident, but too many centers are open only on the usual part-time basis, i.e., six hours a day, or less, if classes are scheduled. Punahou's center is open from 7:30 A.M. to 4:30 P.M. daily.

Fortunately, you do not need a million dollars to design and build an effective media center. Of course, financial support can make the task of building a center easy, but the *principles* that make the Punahou center superior should be considered regardless of the money available.

4

Teaching Teachers: Developing Innovative Training and In-Service Programs for Administrators and Staff

The Challenge of Media Training: Suggested Procedures

The preservice and in-service training of teachers in the effective use of media in the classroom have not resulted in the improvement of instruction because of traditional obstacles. These obstacles include a formidable list of personal and organizational resistance factors that are difficult to overcome:

1. *Fear of the New or the Unknown.*—Both teacher candidates and teachers often feel uncomfortable and insecure with new materials and techniques that vary markedly from the way they have been taught.

2. *Fear of the Mechanical.*—Both teacher candidates and teachers (especially women who have been taught to believe that they are not mechanically or technically oriented) believe that they will never learn how to use media equipment and supplies.

3. *Lack of Professional Acceptance.*—The mistaken belief of university professors and administrators, supervisors and administrators and teachers themselves that knowledge and use of media was sub-professional or

technical retarded the growth of media courses and cadres of professionals who could train teachers and trainers.

4. *Lack of Financial Resources.*—The cost of equipment, supplies and additional specialists on teaching staffs has slowed the growth of media training programs.

5. *Resistance of Decision Makers and Other Groups.*—Administrators, librarians and teacher groups have resisted the advance of media technology, primarily because of a lack of understanding with respect to its use and instructional value.

Fortunately, these attitudes have softened because of a growing number of courses in colleges and universities, recognition of the value of communication and media by state departments and teacher groups, the favorable attitudes toward the work of visual and audio artists, cinemaphotographers, communications authorities, and the general acceptance of multiple media by the public and the younger generation who intuitively recognized the teaching impact of media.

The growth of teacher training is detailed in the next section.

Types of Teacher Training

State departments and universities have increased professional requirements and courses at an accelerated pace since 1940 when the first graduate course in audiovisual education was offered at Indiana University during the summer session. By 1946 that university approved an integrated program of graduate courses in audiovisual education leading to a major for the master's and doctoral levels. Ten years later the Indiana Graduate Division described fourteen graduate courses carrying a total of 44 semester hours of credit in their 1956–57 bulletin.[1] That institution is now considering a two-year program for the specialist's degree and a third year for doctoral students with emphasis on research and development.[2]

Counseling guidelines are currently under development at Indiana University's Audiovisual Center to include such important planning tools as ". . . the rationale, recommended entry requirements, career objectives and professional positions, desired competencies, and the recommended major and inside and outside minor courses suggested for the master's, specialist's and doctoral degree levels." [3]

---

[1] L. C. Larson, "Developing an Integrated College Audiovisual Program," *Phi Delta Kappan,* 38 (February, 1957), pp. 211–21. (L. C. Larson is associate dean and director, Audiovisual Center, Indiana University, Bloomington.)

[2] L. C. Larson, "Developing a Graduate Program to Train Instructional Design and Media Specialists," *Audiovisual Instruction* (January, 1969), pp. 22, 23.

[3] *Ibid.,* p. 24.

Photo 9. State departments of education have increased professional requirements for media specialists while providing increasing aid to local districts for media experimentation and use. (Photograph courtesy of Lee E. Campion, Director, Division of Educational Communications, New York State Education Department.)

Survey research completed at the Educational Media Center of Temple University established the following model professional preparation program based on criteria for determining the role of educational media personnel.

I. General requirements for media personnel
   A. A bachelor's degree
   B. A valid elementary or secondary teaching certificate
   C. Three years of successful professional experience at the elementary or secondary school level

II. Specific requirements for media personnel
   A. Requirements for elementary and secondary building coordinators
      1. Three hours—selection, utilization, manipulation, and evaluation of media materials and hardware
      2. Three hours—psychology and theories of learning
      3. Three hours—design and preparation of media materials

      4. Plus nine hours to be selected from the following:
        a. Graphics production
        b. Internship
        c. Library science
        d. Supervision of instruction and curriculum development
        e. Administration of media
  B. Requirements for media specialists
      1. Three hours—selection, utilization, manipulation, and evaluation of media materials and hardware
      2. Three hours—psychology and theories of learning
      3. Three hours—design and preparation of media materials
      4. Three hours—administration of media services
      5. Three hours—supervision of instruction and curriculum development
      6. Plus fifteen hours to be selected from the following:
        a. Introduction to instructional television
        b. Educational film and video tape production
        c. Photographic techniques in education
        d. Introduction to computer-assisted instruction
        e. Graphics production
        f. Internship
        g. Programed learning
        h. Library science [4]

Nearly every teacher preparation institution in the country now provides or requires some course work in communications, educational technology or the use of media in the instructional process. At the University of Tennessee, for example, an experimental four-year professional education sequence is under development that includes unique self-instructional modules with appropriate planning for media use:

    Behavioral Objectives
    Evaluation of Learning
    Planning for Teaching
    Organizing for Instruction
    Curriculum Development and Evaluation
    Selection and Use of Audiovisual Materials
    Operation of Audiovisual Equipment
    Use of the Library

---

[4] Bill F. Grady, "The Preparation and Certification of Educational Media Personnel," *Audiovisual Instruction* (January, 1969), p. 29.

Research Literacy
Diagnosing of Learning Difficulties
Teaching the Disadvantaged [5]

Another college at the University of Bridgeport (Connecticut) has integrated media instruction into existing methods courses during a three-year sequence beginning at the sophomore level. This college of education program assumes four objectives for preservice teachers:

1. knowledge of the values of good educational communication;
2. competency in the selection, utilization and evaluation of instructional media;
3. experiences in the production of simple-to-make audiovisual materials; and
4. skill in the operation of audiovisual devices.[6]

A third model that extends or improves the training of preservice teachers has been developed by the New York State Teacher Reserve Center at Long Island University's Graduate School of Education. The Center has bridged the school-university gap with an unusual "on-location" preservice project for prospective teachers with bachelor's degrees. In this program, every methods class, plus some other courses (child psychology, contemporary philosophy of education, principles and practices of guidance, remedial reading, the emotionally disturbed child and the culturally different child) are taught *entirely* in the local public schools. Candidates work with children in their natural educational environment where they observe the behavior of children when the usual variety of imposing factors play havoc with the normal classroom day.[7]

Recognizing the need for practical training in multimedia techniques, the LIU center developed a course that utilized an "on-site" Mobile Instruction Media Center (MIMC) for its intensive and highly practical media course. The MIMC was developed by The Education Council (TEC), which is the research and development division of the Nassau County (New York) Board of Cooperative Educational Services, under an ESEA Title III grant from the USOE. (See chapter 5 for a detailed description of the MIMC project.) An outline of that course emphasizing communications

---

[5] Donald L. Haefele, "Self-Instruction and Teacher Education," *Audiovisual Instruction* (January, 1969), p. 63.

[6] George E. Ingham, "Preservice Media Training," *Audiovisual Instruction* (January, 1969), pp. 55, 56.

[7] Rita Stafford Dunn, "Continuing Education Comes of Age," *Journal of the National Association of Women Deans and Counselors,* Vol. 32, No. 3 (Spring, 1969), p. 140.

and the practical problems encountered by teachers in utilizing media follows:

COMMUNICATIONS MEDIA IN CONTEMPORARY EDUCATION: INSTRUCTIONAL MATERIALS IN THE CLASSROOM OF TODAY

Description

Selection, production and use of media materials in teaching and learning at all levels of education; attention to films, filmstrips, slides, transparencies, tapes and recordings, radio and television, and programed instruction.

Objectives

To utilize books and media materials in the promotion of learning

To discover how the various media improve teaching and develop communication skills and understandings

To practice selecting, evaluating, producing, and using media materials.

Outline of Course Content

I. The Communications Revolution
   A. The impact of visual and aural means of communication on contemporary society and culture
   B. The role of the senses in learning
   C. How the various media can be used to promote learning
II. The Information Explosion
   A. Implications for the curriculum
   B. Emphasis on process and discovery rather than content
   C. Role of the library in the school as a communications and learning center
      1. Individualizing instruction through the use of a wide variety of materials
      2. The study carrel; student use of materials
III. Using Communications Media in the Classroom
   A. Identification of materials, sources, review media, and standards of selection
   B. Preparation, use and evaluation of materials
      1. Operation of equipment
      2. Printed materials (books, paperbacks, pamphlets, periodicals)
      3. Media materials (films, filmstrips, slides, transparencies, pictures, film loops, recordings, tapes)
   C. Programed instruction

        1. Background and philosophy
        2. Production and use
    D. Demonstration lessons on use of materials

Two examples of how regional media centers have been designed to solve the problem of in-service teacher training may be found at the Texas State University and the Granite, Utah, school district.

The statewide Texas training program is designed for teachers from districts that have very *limited* media programs. It was established to train teachers in the use of materials and to implement more effective media usage in their home districts. The Granite, Utah, program is for teachers from schools that have made *extensive* use of media materials for years.

The three-week program operated through the Texas State University system has three phases.

During phase one, the skills that might be used profitably by classroom teachers are emphasized—dry mounting, laminating, lettering, layout skills for the production of posters, bulletin boards and mounted photos. (Orientation to these skills is important even where graphics technicians and aides are employed to assist teachers.)

In phase two, the use, evaluation and preparation of projectable materials are emphasized. Instruction covers overhead projection systems, commercially prepared transparencies, films and filmstrips, 35mm equipment and slides, 8mm photography, and general techniques for creating and using these instructional media.

The week-long session begins with teachers learning the basics of 35mm photography—how to take a good picture. The teachers are given enough practical information and training for preparing good materials without turning the course into a highly technical session. Each of the teacher-students then produces a 35mm slide presentation covering a specific classroom subject.

As for 8mm instruction, each participant is taught how to judge lighting, to make a story board and to shoot and time sequences.

Finally, the class is divided into camera crews to produce a single-concept film. This process of actually making a film proves especially valuable when the teachers evaluate commercial materials for their own districts.

In phase three, participants are encouraged to set up a "pilot school" to demonstrate an effective media program in their districts. The latest listing indicates that, so far, more than fifty such schools have been established.

As indicated previously, the program operating in the Granite, Utah, district is primarily designed to give new teachers an *orientation* to the use of media materials. It is very similar, in content, to the Texas project, but it includes training in more sophisticated media and materials.

The Granite program comprises twelve three-hour sessions (one a week). Granite has a new instructional media center with extensive facilities, including a recording studio, photographic darkrooms, a print shop and other sophisticated equipment for the use of the district's teachers. New teachers are trained in the use of these facilities and equipment in their own classrooms and schools.

New York State's Department of Education and the State University of New York (SUNY) have developed "A Multimedia Course in Instructional Technology for Teachers."

This instructional course has been designed and developed for utilization either by school districts and boards of cooperative educational services as an in-service course for teachers, or by institutions of higher education as a basis for a college credit course.

Photo 10. The course will include materials for various instructional activities such as . . . laboratory activities. . . . (Photograph used with permission of the publisher of *School Management* Magazine, copyright 1968, 1969, Management Publishing Group, Inc.)

The course includes materials for various instructional activities, such as lecture-presentations, group discussions, laboratory activities, and self-study. Major emphasis has been placed upon the effective utilization of multimedia presentations in order to provide the student with practical methods of instruction. Universities and other educational institutions throughout the state have assisted with the enterprise.

This ambitious project emphasized behavioral objectives, affective factors, systems, research, the characteristics of media, instructional change, and practical applications. The approach appears to be current, comprehensive and relevant for teachers in training or in-service work. New teachers are trained in the use of these facilities and equipment in their own classrooms and schools.

Critical Guidelines for In-Service Programs

Impressive advances made by the teacher and specialist preparation institutions and centers seem to parallel the accelerated pace of technological development in industry, the military and society in general. Many educators could argue, however, that preparation for specialists and the utilization of media in the classrooms have been outstripped by industry, from here to the moon; a distance now easily managed by space ships and clear, beautiful color television pictures.

Part of the problem, of course, is priority of funding. Federal expenditures for defense and the space program have been astronomical compared with allocations for education. Whether funds increase or not, critical guidelines for effective media training programs should be developed within each school district or building to improve teacher and media specialist performance. As noted earlier, the colleges and universities have gradually improved the preparation of media personnel. The suggested guidelines that follow, therefore, are concerned with in-service training and professional growth at the local school level.

Professional growth for teachers and administrators should be:

1. *Self-Motivating;*
   It is essential that teachers be involved in the planning of their in-service work so that they can perceive potential and actual "payoffs" in self-growth. These rewards may take the form of an increased ability to hold student interest through more exciting teaching lessons, increased student comprehension through auditory and visual sensory appeal, or through more effective evaluations. Moreover, current teacher interest in status and participation in decisions that affect them is irreversible. Planning for one's self-improvement is consistent with this trend.

2. *Continuous;*
   Rapid advances in knowledge, technology and communication, and signs of revolutionary changes in the society—e.g., teacher, parent, and student involvement in decision making, and the advancing role of minorities in the power structure and the problems of poverty

and pollution—mandate continuous growth by the educational establishment. Survival of our society is literally dependent on continuous adaptation and growth.

3. *Individualized;*

It may seem obvious that in-service courses should be designed to meet the individual needs of the teachers in the program. Not so apparent to many is the need to consider the individual needs of the students who presumably will benefit from the continuous growth of teachers and administrators. In general, in-service courses follow standard patterns, e.g., philosophy and practice, "practical" workshops, administration and supervision, technological tools and systems theory, to name but a few that are applied to in-service in educational technology. Programs should be designed with direct concern for the teachers involved and with relevance for the selected students they serve in a given setting at a specific time.

4. *Flexible;*

If in-service courses are to be self-motivated, continuous and individualized, they must be allowed to break the "credit barrier" and the usual rigid, inflexible procedures. For example, personnel regulations might dictate that for a teacher to achieve two credits on the salary scale past the master's level, he "must attend a minimum of thirteen sessions of fifteen," report at a specific time every Thursday and complete all of the forms and requirements necessary for standard college course work. If what individual teachers need by way of professional growth in their personal situations can be determined and provided by the in-service design, credits might then be allowed for growth— not endurance. Under such circumstances behavioral change for the better and not reinforcement of the status quo might become a reality, and independent effort—not group mediocrity—might become increasingly evident.

5. *Self-Fulfilling;*

There may be no greater opportunity to reach self-fulfillment professionally than through in-service growth. Self-renewal, higher individual expectations, personal excitement, and long-term rewards can be achieved by teachers who are provided with (a) opportunities to participate directly in the development of the in-service design, (b) exciting, stimulating sessions, (c) flexible schedules and programs, and (d) relevant materials and techniques.

A Simple In-Service Course for a School Building

Teachers need to understand and to touch, to use and to improvise with media tools if they are to realize their potential. Elementary teachers are usually fearful of introducing science equipment, materials and chemicals into the classroom until they have had practice in using them. The same is true for media equipment and materials.

Begin by involving the teachers in a planning session to organize a media in-service course that will benefit all teachers in the building. Include basic instructional elements and appropriate time segments convenient to all. One sample course the staff might develop would be based on fifteen sessions spread over the school year:

I.	Why Use Media? Sample Demonstrations:	1 session
II.	Selection and Use of Media Equipment:	2 sessions
III.	Selection and Use of Media Materials:	4 sessions
IV.	Evaluation of Media Equipment Materials:	4 sessions
V.	Practical Relationships to Learning:	4 sessions
VI.	Sharing Effective Experiences at Each Session Beginning with III:	13 sessions

This introductory course will insure that teachers are familiar with and able to use equipment and materials and that they share good teaching techniques. It will aid a school staff in examining its objectives and teaching patterns and may stimulate the staff to request the more sophisticated and individualized types of clinics and team approaches to the use of media that are described in the following sections.

Photo 11. In-service courses should be self-motivating. . . . (Photograph courtesy of Fountain Valley School District, Fountain Valley, California.)

Practical Clinics for Administrators and Teachers:
Breaking the Credit Barrier

One technique gaining wide acceptance for in-service education is the practical clinic. If professional growth is to be self-motivating, continuous, individualized, flexible, and self-fulfilling, then what better vehicle than a flexible set of sessions initiated and planned by the participants with assistance from top professionals, university personnel and expert coordinators?

Clinics, and all good in-service programs, for that matter, are developed out of felt and expressed needs because similar offerings are not provided by local colleges and universities or the school district. Further, good in-service programs can offer continuing rewards in the form of materials, special publications, teaching units, lesson plans and demonstrations, audio and video tapes, bibliographies, annotated booklets, transparencies, slides, and teachers' guides. The specific questions of individuals can be answered, and the sharing of experiences can result in concrete action procedures. For example, the sincere teacher who bemoans his or her lack of knowledge concerning the utilization of transparencies can see demonstrations and learn the principles involved in building a lesson through the use of sequential overlays by "doing it herself" with other participants in the clinic. All of the principles of learning, such as motivation, transfer of training and reinforcement, and the provision of sociopsychological self-renewal experiences, can take place under these conditions. The participants are all in "the same boat" with the insecurity or fear of an actual situation removed.

Clinics can be of maximum benefit if several schools or school districts are involved. The "regional approach" provides additional resources, increases the number of participants with varying backgrounds and experiences and adds a professional tone without over-structuring the program. A series of clinics and workshops was developed regionally for Nassau County, New York, by The Education Council (TEC) as a result of inquiries and requests from teachers and administrators. Their statements included:

> As an elementary school principal, I no longer know what to look for, or even what I'm looking *at,* when I observe a "modern" math lesson. Can you focus my attention properly?
> I'm a new teacher, and I wasn't given a single clue in college about how to teach division as "repeated subtraction." Where can I begin?
> My students have had difficulty with fractions. The "new math" confuses them as much as the old math when it comes to opera-

tions with common fractions. I'm afraid to show them decimal fractions. What can I do about it?

One series of mathematics workshops and clinics was designed to cover a wide range of problem areas. It was publicized as shown below:

TEC's in-service symbol is composed of circles, squares, and tri angles—ancient symbols of continuity, creative intellect, and order.

One of THE EDUCATION COUNCIL's objectives is the development of dynamic and meaningful in-service programs which will bring creative experiences to classroom teachers. The courses are based on requests from teachers and administrators and are developed because similar courses are not offered by local school districts or by universities. The services of professionals-in-residence, as well as special publications and creative teaching units for the use of individual schools or groups of schools, have resulted from these programs.

FALL WORKSHOPS — NEW TEACHERS

Workshops intended to help introduce new teachers (also substitute teachers) to fundamental concepts regarding the methodology of a "modern" program in elementary school mathematics.

Intermediate Grades Workshop

WHEN: Saturday, September 16, 1967 from 9:30-3:30 p.m.
WHERE: Little Theatre, East Meadow High School, Carman Avenue, East Meadow.
CONTENT: Fundamental concepts regarding the methodology of a "modern" program in elementary school mathematics; use of the TEC *Mathematics Series Course Outlines* and other sources of assistance; adaptation of a textbook series to the TEC curriculum.

Primary Grades Workshop

WHEN: Saturday, September 23, 1967 from 9:30-3:30 p.m.
WHERE: Little Theatre, East Meadow High School, Carman Avenue, East Meadow.
CONTENT: Fundamental concepts regarding the methodology of a "modern" program in elementary school mathematics; use of the TEC Mathematics Series and other sources of assistance; adaptation of a textbook series to the TEC curriculum; use of manipulative materials in the primary grades.

■ ■

FALL CLINICS

Administrators' Clinic

A clinic for elementary administrators and district curriculum leaders. Registration limited to 30.

CONTENT: Overview of major mathematical concepts in K-6; trends in elementary school mathematics; what to look for in a mathematics lesson; organizing a faculty for a modern mathematics program.
DATES: Tuesdays, September 19, 26, October 3, 10, and 17.
TIME: 10:30 a.m.-12:00 noon.
PLACE: Irving J. Baylis School, Woodbury Road, Syosset, New York.
Note: TEC will supply competent personnel who will partially structure the clinic sessions and will serve as resource persons in the area(s) under discussion. However, emphasis will be on interaction among experienced educators.

Teaching Fractions Clinic • Grades 4-6
A clinic for classroom teachers who are responsible for presenting mathematics in grades 4-6.

CONTENT:	Subject matter and methodology related to the teaching of fractions in common form, grades 4-6. The discussion will include adaptation of various text series in order to implement the program outlined in the TEC *Mathematics Series Course Outline 4-6*.
DATES:	Tuesdays, September 26, October 3, 10, 17, and 24.
TIME:	4:00-5:30 p.m.
PLACE:	Corona Avenue School, Valley Stream, New York.
Note:	This clinic will be repeated in November and December at a site selected to service the districts located in the northeastern section of the county.

The workshops and clinics will be under the supervision of Dr. Hamilton S. Blum, Associate Professor of Mathematics at C. W. Post College and mathematics consultant to THE EDUCATION COUNCIL.

▲ ▲▲

Although taken from only one subject matter discipline, several principles and procedures used in developing the modern mathematics in-service series could be utilized in developing clinics for professional growth in the use of media:

1. Use the relevant questions and suggestions of the participant "consumers" in planning and building the course with them.

2. Regionalize to provide a broader base of resources and experience.

3. Provide group sessions according to need, grade levels, subject matter, experience, roles in school, and critical problem areas.

4. Allow the substance of the clinic to determine its structure and content, unrestricted by credit requirements. Seek prior approval of salary credit if given under inflexible policies that legislate Carnegie units or the college credit approach. As a matter of fact, many universities are now experimenting with independent study, reports instead of grades, and student involvement in curriculum development. At any rate, break the credit barrier to professional growth.

Microteaching and the Minicourse

Teachers who can see and hear themselves conducting a discussion lesson have a tremendous tool for self-improvement. Some teachers lecture seventy per cent of the time. Many may repeat their questions fourteen times in a twenty-minute lesson. A few teachers repeat pupils' answers thirty-one times in the same interval. In such situations, no comment by a supervisor can effectively equal a video tape reviewing of a lesson. The use of video tape recorder equipment (VTR) may prove to be of tremendous value to administrators and teachers in their efforts to improve instruction.

Photo 12. Teachers who can see and hear themselves conducting a discussion lesson have a tremendous tool for self-improvement. (Photograph courtesy of Shaver & Company, Architects, Salina, Kansas.)

The Suffolk County, New York, Regional Center for Supplementary Educational Services utilized microteaching techniques [8] in conjunction with a minicourse [9] incorporated into a structured in-service course for teachers. The object of the program was to assist teachers in developing improved teaching patterns after seeing a few twenty-minute samples of themselves in action in a classroom.

A building principal, a coordinator, a media technician, and several teachers participated directly in the project. The principal involved teachers and consulted with the coordinator and technician in scheduling building space and equipment.

The coordinator and the media technician aided teachers by training them in the use of VTR equipment, e.g., adjustment of video levels, audio levels, camera, tape switches, video receiver, and video recorder. This training constituted the first part of the in-service program. Both the coordinator and the technician also had responsibility for facilities, pre- and

---

[8] A course in self-operation and analysis of video taped lessons developed by Stanford University in California for use with teaching interns and small groups of students.

[9] A series of instructional films and video tapes evolved by the Far West Laboratory for Educational Research and Development to teach learning skills, effective questioning, peer tutoring, etc.

post-testing of teachers, and arrangement for repair of equipment through a servicing company.

Teachers were selected for attitudes and flexibility and were provided released time in order to take the course during the school day. One substitute teacher covered the classes of four teachers during microteaching sessions for seventy-five minutes of released time each day for fifteen days.

The coordinator became essential to the success of the project. Breakdowns of equipment, substitution of equipment, the solution of human relations problems, scheduling, and generally following through required competent leadership and coordination.

The four intermediate teachers who conducted the microteaching demonstration project in the Suffolk Center used randomly selected groups of five to eight children from their own classes. For the first two days the teachers saw an introductory film describing the new approach and its advantages. They then prepared a lesson involving questioning as a demonstration skill. The teachers gave this practice lesson to their entire class, and the lesson was filmed on video tape for future information. Subsequently, teachers viewed an instructional film explaining three questioning techniques and then a model film demonstrating how another teacher used the skills being taught. Teachers then prepared a short lesson based on current classwork, applying the recently acquired skills. Teachers studied these individual video tapes for overall effect, not for close analysis. Immediately afterward, a second viewing (both were private) was held with other teachers assisting on the evaluations. The evaluations formed the basis for the preparation of new lessons that were video taped for post evaluation. These steps were repeated for each segment of the course.

The dependent variable data that were accumulated in the evaluation sessions included:

1. Percentage of discussion time taken by teacher talk.
2. Number of times teacher used redirection.
3. Number of times teacher used prompting.
4. Number of times teacher used further clarification.
5. Number of times teacher used refocusing.
6. Number of times teacher repeated his/her own questions.
7. Number of times teacher repeated pupils' answers.
8. Number of times teacher answered his/her own questions.
9. Length of pupil responses in words (based on five-minute samples of pre- and post-tapes).
10. Number of one-word pupil responses (based on five-minute samples of pre- and post-tapes).

11. Length of teacher's pause after question (based on five-minute samples of pre- and post-tapes).

12. Frequency of punitive teacher reactions to incorrect pupil answers.

13. Percentage of total questions that called for high-level cognitive pupil responses.

Teachers in the Suffolk district reduced "teacher talking" from fifty-eight to thirty-five per cent. "Redirection" (the technique of framing questions so that the question is directed to several pupils rather than one) increased fifty per cent. Teacher repetition of questions was reduced by more than one-half, and the length of pupil responses increased by commensurate amounts.

In the comments contained in the Suffolk County Regional Center's report, all teachers believed that the microteaching and minicourse technique had immense value for the experienced teacher; none doubted its in-service value. The only criticism recorded was of a minor nature and focused on technical details of the video tape equipment.

To summarize, the first month of the course was devoted to pre-testing and use of equipment and facilities. The second month included introduction, practice sessions and four instructional sequences. The last month was designed for a final instructional sequence and post-testing. Self- and group evaluation increased as the course progressed. Basic equipment for the program included:

    1 projector, 16mm
    1 portable screen on tripod
    1 TV camera, viewfinder w/zoom and wide-angle lens
    1 camera tripod w/dolly and spring head
    2 microphones
    1 microphone mixer
    2 video recorders
    1 educational TV receiver-monitor
    1 stand for TV receiver-monitor
    1 cart for VTR w/attached cord, miscellaneous cables and connectors
    4 flood lights w/clamp-type holders, extension cords, miscellaneous
      items or repair tools, cleaning implements
   10 video tape, 1″ size, 1 hour per reel
    1 portable TV receiver-monitor

Some of the equipment needed is now standard in many schools. A few additions and careful planning might make microteaching a reality in most educationally alert districts.

How to Individualize Media In-Service Training

There is nothing quite as incongruous as a media lecture or program without the use of media itself. There is no excuse for a *lecture* on educational technology. At the other extreme is the use of media tools without purpose. The classic story, in this regard, concerns the college professor who taped all of his lectures from ancient yellow notes so that he could travel and consult while his students listened to his "canned" presentations. By accident the professor found himself on his own campus one day and decided to visit his classroom. There he found his tape spinning according to schedule. But the students were gone and in their seats were 200 tape machines recording every golden phrase.

Somewhere between these two extremes are the realistic everyday problems of teachers who require assistance in the use of media to improve instruction. Individualizing in-service work for teachers can be approached through the workshops and clinics noted earlier in this chapter. Continuing work and follow-up sessions must be provided at the local building level, however, if the teacher or administrator is to effect meaningful behavioral changes in the instructional program.

Some specific techniques for individualizing in-service work at the building level include provision of:

Photo 13. Individualizing in-service work. (Photograph courtesy of Fountain Valley School District, Fountain Valley, California.)

1. Building clinics with "booths" or tables for individual teachers to meet and consult with expert media specialists or teachers.

2. Team planning sessions with other teachers, aides, and specialists in assigning individual tasks for media presentations.

3. Independent study opportunities for teachers or administrators using a variety of media, both print and non-print.

4. Pilot tryouts and preparation sessions by individual teachers assisted by two or three interested and able students.

5. A library-instructional materials center used by teachers and administrators.

6. Staff or team workshops to develop materials and presentations to solve individual instructional problems.

There are advantages, too, in building a resource library of media materials and aids to the teacher on an individualized basis:

1. The teacher or administrator has instant access to individualized materials for self-growth at times when he or she is ready for the next step, not according to a rigid course schedule.

2. Resources for individual instructional courses are available in conjunction with the advice of those who prepared them for use.

3. An available, constantly expanding school library of self-training materials reduces the effort to obtain appropriate materials and make them operational.

4. Recordings of visiting consultants and professionals can be utilized by individual teachers and students who did not hear or see the original performance.

5. Sections and fragments of tapes or films can be utilized to serve particular needs of teachers, administrators and students.

The current drive to individualize instruction should have been preceded by individualized in-service training. Most school systems are seeking ways to adopt systems that are not in harmony with the understandings and experiences of the staff. The judicious use of a wide range of media offers numerous opportunities to individualize instruction for teachers, administrators and students, even if they have had no prior experiences in this field.

In-Service for Media Teams—Teachers and Aides

A major drawback in many training and improvement programs for educational personnel is poor communication among the various educator-specialists and a consequent restriction on the exchange of ideas for improving classroom teaching practices. In spite of the fact that many suggestions for instructional improvement are available in the literature and from the experiences of various professional specialists, and although school librarians and media specialists occupy central roles in the development and implementation of new teaching strategies, professional assistance is often unused simply because practical channels of communication with the classroom teacher are not made available.

One Educational Personnel Development Act (EPDA) institute communicated the professional expertise of media specialists and librarians to classroom teachers through in-service training provided by a three-member specialist team, consisting of a master teacher, a media specialist or a librarian and one auxiliary aide (technician-trainee).[10] The use and training of teams, as suggested in this project, merges the efforts of two professional educators with a paraprofessional, or teacher aide. The team approach to instructional improvement has received only limited attention thus far in teacher education, yet advances in this area may well provide not only new patterns for teacher training but also a model for in-service programs of cooperation and communication among teachers, media specialists or librarians, and teacher aides, or technicians.

It was the major objective of the project outlined below to demonstrate improvement in instruction by training fifteen three-member specialist teams to assist classroom teachers in the refinement of teaching practices and materials.

The teams' task will be to introduce advances in the utilization of educational technology that (for a variety of reasons) have been slow to be adopted by the schools. The teams will seek to overcome the natural reluctance of classroom teachers to give up supposedly "tried and true" traditional methods and overcome their fear of "new" equipment. The teams can make inroads on the frequent unavailability of instructional materials and provide them when and where they are needed.

The teams will also attempt to correct: (1) the lack of facilities and equipment for generating materials for a particular teaching purpose, (2) the lack of trained staff for making educational media easily accessible, (3) general teacher unawareness of what the media center-library can offer in implementing the instructional program, and (4) lack of teacher motivation to change and improve teaching procedures.

---

[10] "Teams for Advancing Teacher Training in Use of Instructional Resources," USOE #OEG–0–9–424396–2121–725 (Proposal for Educational Personnel Development Grant, The Education Council, New York, 1969).

TYPICAL SCHEDULE: INSTITUTE WEEK

Day	Morning Session	Afternoon Session	Evening
Monday	Common presentation or demonstration Tech (Technician) MS (Media Specialist) TT (Teacher-Trainer)	Tech: Lab Practice TT: Group Seminar MS: Evaluation Workshop	Independent Study
Tuesday	Selected field trips to schools with innovative media programs, school media centers and commercial producers of instructional materials and educational technology products		Independent Study
Wednesday	Visiting Lecturer: Curriculum development and innovations Small-group discussions and clinic sessions	Visiting Lecturer: Question and answer period—further discussion	Independent Study
Thursday	Team study and planning sessions (15 teams of 3)	Lab workshop (team and individual practice as required)	Independent Study
Friday	Sample team multimedia presentation	1. Lab practice session 2. Individual study	Independent Study

Disciplines and Fields of Study

The disciplines and fields of study on which the training was based were library science—technical and clerical procedures, school library services to professional staff; education methods and materials—elementary schools; curriculum development—reading-language arts, social studies, science, mathematics, health education; communications—use of equipment or materials, and evaluation of media. Visiting "presentors" supplemented the institute staff in the exploration of these disciplines and aspects of teaching methods.

PROGRAM OF SUMMER INSTITUTE

1. *The School Media Center*
   a. Philosophy—communications revolution, need for variety of media

    b. Contents—films, filmstrips, records, tapes, film loops, transparencies, etc.

    c. Applications—the media center in the teaching program

2. *Roles of Team Members*

    a. Learning tasks

    b. Service tasks in the school

    c. Instructional tasks

3. *Communication in Education*

    a. Understanding communication theory

    b. Utilization of media in the process of communicating information, concepts and attitudes

TASKS LEARNED AND PERFORMED BY INSTITUTE PARTICIPANTS		
Technician	*Media Specialist or Librarian*	*Teacher-Trainer*
Operation and maintenance of media and graphics equipment (intensive study and practice)	Operation and maintenance of media and graphics equipment (overview and general introduction)	Operation and maintenance of media and graphics equipment (overview and introduction)
Technical processing of books and media	Technical processing of books and media	Technical processing of books and media
Covering, labeling, pasting pockets, mounting transparencies and slides	Cataloging of non-book materials	
Typing and filing of cards		
(Intensive study and practice)	(Intensive study and practice)	(Overview—to provide basic understanding of library technology)
Graphics production	Graphics production	Graphics production
Operation of duplicating equipment, diazo transparency	Operation of duplicating equipment, diazo transparency	Operation of duplicating equipment, diazo transparency
Tape duplication	Tape duplication	Tape duplication
(Intensive study and practice)	(Intensive study and practice)	(Intensive study and practice)
Designing of materials not commercially available	Evaluation of non-book materials	Role of media center in school programs

Technician	Media Specialist or Librarian	Teacher-Trainer
	Selection of tools and review of media	
	Incorporation of new media in the traditional library	Use of new media in the instructional program
Location and delivery of materials to user	Selection of media for use in solving teacher problems	Solution of problems in teaching with media
	Identification of teacher needs	Independent use of library tools
Elementary school curriculum (overview)	Changing emphasis in elementary school curriculum	Changing emphasis in elementary school curriculum
	Lectures in major subject areas: language arts social studies science mathematics	Lectures in major subject areas: language arts social studies science mathematics
Library clerical procedures		
Maintenance of records		
Filing of order cards, catalog cards, vertical file		
Shelving of books and media materials		
Typing of purchase orders		
Inventory		

This team approach is designed to spread to dozens of school districts in phases. Increased media effectiveness was noted as interrelationships among participants developed and expanded. This was evidenced in the following ways:

1. Working together on common problems improved relationships among specialist team members who developed new understandings of each other's problems and recognition of mutual goals. Indeed, the team seemed much better able to solve problems than individual team members.

2. Teacher-to-teacher dialogue increased, and a new medium for exchange of ideas and professional insights was created.

3. The selection process for acquiring and using instructional media was improved through guided study of criteria and practical application.

4. Accessibility of instructional media was enhanced by the employment of technician-clerks, the retraining of professional library personnel and the increased acceptance of the team's professional role by other teachers, local administrators, and boards of education.

5. The variety and utilization of materials was expanded through teacher contact with new ideas and programs.

6. Short- and long-range planning for acquisition and use of materials replaced, to a large degree, the frequently haphazard procedures that previously existed.

7. Evidence of improved results was verified by disadvantaged students and students from affluent areas who frequently attack "irrelevant teaching methods and content."

In summary, the total effect achieved by this team in-service project was the enhancement of the teaching process and the improvement of learning.

Tips for Planning and Implementing Change: From Human Relations to Floor Plans

Whether you are a teacher, a media specialist, a librarian, an administrator, or a board member, human relations skills are essential in bringing about positive change. Certain principles apply, and even after significant change is made, "back sliding" to older, more established habit patterns often washes away much of the progress made by a forward-looking school or district.

Tremendous gains made in the teaching of "modern math" through massive in-service programs have often been modified by a return to straight "drill" procedures because "computation skills have fallen off." In the media field, an "overhead projector" in every classroom has resulted too often in obtaining a "dust catcher" in most classrooms. Perhaps even worse is the "I have a headache today; which films are still available?" approach to teaching with media.

Certain principles have been demonstrated by practitioners in industry and observers in social psychology, but too often they are ignored by those seeking to bring about change:

1. The person affected by change must be considered the consumer to whom a process is being sold. He must have a strong voice in the decisions that affect him. Of more importance, he should be directly involved in the change that affects him from the inception of the idea to its implementation, evaluation and eventual modifications.

2. The change must be consistent with the consumer's frame of reference, whether it is a classroom, a desk, a library, an office, the other teachers in his department or grade level, the subject he teaches, or the types of students assigned to him.

3. There must be a "payoff," or reward, that the consumer enjoys, whether it is additional compensation, increased status, enhanced prestige, improved self-image, personal recognition, self-fulfillment, career advances, productive preparations, happier classroom climate, improved learning patterns, or more self-involvement for stimulating teaching.

4. Change cannot be wrought without considerable care and planning. Sensitivity to the importance of proper timing, accuracy and quality of presentations, sincerity of intent, correct definition of the problem, candor by all involved in the change, communication, consolidation of gains, and reinforcement of positive patterns can mean the difference between success and failure.

Those who study organizations and men at work offer helpful patterns. One group of social scientists suggests the problem-solving approach for members of different groups such as teachers, administrators, media specialists, and librarians: [11]

For example, one sequence designed to foster change through involvement might begin with a *joint meeting* of the groups concerned in an effort to describe a *joint task*. After *review* of the task and analysis of *alternate procedures,* the group might *test* the *alternate solutions* and then share in the *outcome.*[12]

Another expert at "human engineering" suggests seven interaction guidelines for planning change:

1. Develop a perception of "equality" among those considering solutions to a problem. [This is sometimes called "symbolic equality" or "temporary power equalization."]

2. Attack the man who isn't there. [A strawman, scapegoat or even a terrible facility can be attacked to build rapport.]

3. Encourage full expression of true feelings. [This is safe sensitivity-training activity.]

4. Build a pattern of agreement. [Use minor points first if necessary.]

5. Use safety valves such as humor to release tension.

6. Find personal points in common to build goodwill. [These may be sports, opera, cars, etc.]

---

[11] Despite accelerated recognition and increased cooperation, the last two groups have not yet completely merged. (See chapter 5.)

[12] Based on Robert R. Blake, Herbert A. Shepard and Jane S. Morton, *Managing Intergroup Conflict in Industry* (Houston, Texas: Gulf Publishing Co., 1964), pp. 94–101.

7. Make the operational framework clear. Use clear communication and a friendly, flexible approach.[13]

Whichever approach you use, be sure to involve everyone concerned if you contemplate drawing up plans for an instructional materials center in either an old or a new building with media built into every room. Such designs can be included as part of in-service workshops for teams of teachers and administrators.

---

[13]Based on William Foote Whyte, *Men at Work* (Homewood, Ill.: The Dorsey Press, Inc., and Richard D. Irwin, Inc., 1961), p. 324.

5

Gaining Library - Media
Cooperation to
Improve Instruction

Guidelines for Teachers, Librarians and Administrators

Strong and long overdue attempts to blend the efforts of media personnel and school librarians have met partial success, in practice, across the country. The recently released *Standards for School Media Programs* further merges the complementary roles of the two groups.

The new standards were prepared by a joint committee of the American Association of School Librarians and the Department of Audiovisual Instruction of the National Education Association. The Joint Committee promoted cooperative effort early in the preface of its publication: "When the question of revising standards was first discussed, it became clear that standards for media programs would be greatly strengthened if they were prepared jointly by the two professional associations most closely identified with the resources for teaching and learning in the schools, and issued as a single document." [1]

---

[1] American Association of School Librarians, *Standards for School Media Programs* (Washington, D.C.: Department of Audiovisual Instruction, National Education Association, 1969).

Despite the emphasis being placed upon cooperative development, even the combined efforts of media specialists and librarians may not bring about the improvements recommended by the new standards. A report issued by the Educational Facilities Laboratories pinpointed the obstacles to revisions in school libraries or the conditions that created poor situations:

—A philosophy of education that provides little motivation or time for student use of the library.

—A study hall concept of the library which discourages affection for reading, and turns the library into a forbidding place rather than a living room. Most often the library is too formal, too institutionalized, devoid of pleasant furniture, and lacking in imaginative displays and service.

—A physical setting that is not only isolated from the main stream of student traffic, but is also inadequate in size.

—A collection of books, periodicals, newspapers, and audiovisual materials so small that it stifles potential interests and meets only the needs of the poorest and most limited students in the school.

—A separation of book and audiovisual services.

—A library that fails to take into account the fact that the technology of communication is changing rapidly.

—A lack of understanding by the administration that competent librarians should be delegated the responsibility and authority to administer the library and work with the teaching staff as materials consultants.

—A concept of staff size that limits the librarians' energies and time to the routine tasks, giving them no opportunity to play an intimate role in the instructional program.[2]

In addition to these poor situations, and despite the joint committee on standards, media specialists and librarians remain at odds in too many instances. Logically, they would seem to be natural allies of the classroom teacher for the purpose of improving instruction, but, in practice, they have difficulty communicating their points of view and method of operation to the other group.

The schism is probably the result of several complex attitudes and value patterns which are *perceived* as different by each specialist. To illustrate, media specialists view librarians as jealous keepers or guardians of instructional materials such as books. They too often caricature librarians as

---

[2] Ralph E. Ellsworth and Hobart D. Wagener, *The School Library—Facilities for Independent Study in the Secondary School* (New York: Educational Facilities Laboratories, 1963), pp. 14, 15.

Spartans guarding the door to prevent students from taking out books because they might lose or damage them. The library (to the media specialist) seems to be a silent prison where learning is difficult, if not impossible.

Librarians, on the other hand, too often perceive media specialists as disorganized "Johnny-come-lately's" who would destroy the quality system of the library and dilute the value of the written word with inferior audio-visual techniques.

To begin to overcome these misconceptions, recommended guidelines for teachers, media specialists, librarians, and administrators should be task-oriented and alternately bring the resources of learning into the classrooms and the students into the library-resource center. After an introductory period, students would then proceed to observe and join professional teams in problem-solving situations where media could be utilized. Media technicians and media teams, as discussed in chapter 4, would furnish additional dimensions by using the following guidelines:

Guideline 1.—The learning situation should be designed to include a wide variety of instructional resources that appeal to a variety of senses and interests, such as books, records, tapes, films, filmstrips, programed materials, reference photographs, pamphlets, television, activity materials, and original source items.

Photo 14. The learning situation should include . . . films. . . . (Bell & Howell, Audio Visual Products Division, Chicago, Illinois.)

Photo 15.   The learning situation should include . . . films. . . . (Bell & Howell, Audio Visual Products Division, Chicago, Illinois.)

Guideline 2.—Instructional techniques such as individualized assignments, appropriate group learning and teaching practices, differentiated uses of materials, promulgation of reading and resource lists, and group-developed assessment procedures should be utilized to meet the educational needs of each student.

Guideline 3.—Instructional materials centers and classrooms oriented to utilize media should provide continuing opportunities for inquiry and discovery, self-motivation, independent study, reinforcement, and application of learning to new situations.

Guideline 4.—Teachers, media specialists, librarians, and administrators should seek to provide a wide variety of interaction experiences between individual students and student groups, among students, faculty teams and professionals, and between students and the worlds of work, government, higher education, and the community.

Guideline 5.—Members of educational teams should consider themselves consultants and facilitators who develop, guide, evaluate, and implement innovative methods to meet educational and personal growth needs.

Beginning to Plan Implementation of Positive Guidelines

The implementation of the positive guidelines listed above would be expedited if everyone concerned listed general functions that could be expanded at a later date to include all of the specific job description items required of media personnel in a particular local situation. Eventually local clinics and in-service work would be instituted to diffuse individualized and stimulating use of media throughout the school. Two phases of one year each are suggested as a minimum to implement a media program so that it effectively begins to meet the objectives of the guidelines:

Phase I—Development of Basic Proficiencies

1. Locate instructional materials
2. Create simple materials
3. Use media equipment and production equipment
4. Understand the role of media

Media Specialist and Librarian

1. Catalog instructional media
2. Evaluate, select, and acquire media
3. Develop circulation procedures for media
4. Plan acquisition of materials

Teacher-Trainer

1. Evaluate teacher effectiveness in using media
2. Evaluate commercial and locally developed materials
3. Improve quality of instruction by training teachers in the use of media as part of the instructional program

Technician

1. Process and circulate print and non-print media
2. Prepare graphics as needed and duplicate audio tapes
3. Assist in the development of media presentations beyond the routine level

Phase II—Enrollment of School Staff in In-Service Courses

1. Motivate the use of media—theory and practical rationale
2. Assist in preparing instructional programs utilizing media
3. Offer demonstration and practice in using equipment for projection, sound reproduction, and production of materials

Media Specialist and Librarian

1. Select and acquire media
2. Understand media utilization in implementing curriculum
3. Assist in preparation of multimedia units

Teacher-Trainer

1. Utilize media in the instructional program
2. Assist in preparation of lesson plans
3. Aid in selecting appropriate media for instructional needs

Technician

1. Develop accessibility of media
2. Prepare special teaching materials
   as needed

Moving the Library into the Elementary Classroom

The title of this section is enough to raise the book marks of most librarians right out of their places. Before any procedures for decentralization can be described, librarians generally list the usual logistic justifications for the central storage of books and media materials, e.g.,

1. A larger collection of materials can be accumulated more easily.
2. Accessibility through arrangement and cataloging is more feasible.
3. A trained librarian can be justified more easily.
4. Assistance to students and teachers is more readily supplied.
5. Potential exists for scheduling all classes into the library "learning center," thus justifying costs and efforts in terms of demand and supply.

Photo 16.   Media library corners in the elementary classroom can encourage a love of learning. (Photograph courtesy of West Babylon Schools, West Babylon, New York.)

Media specialists, on the other hand, often complain that the materials of learning are not close to students, where they belong. They claim that books and materials are often more inaccessible from a central source than from a smaller, independent center, for a variety of reasons:

1. The librarian, who is frequently overwhelmed by the quantity of volumes and materials, often becomes more interested in protecting books from damage or loss than in seeing them used. In direct contrast, the classroom teacher, who is more directly concerned with her students and the learning process, will tend to place books and materials in students' hands at the moment of greatest potential for learning.

2. The library staff is so harassed by lack of sufficient professional and clerical assistance that antiquated procedures for accessioning books and materials reduces the amount of professional aid given to teachers and students.

3. Increased demands upon elementary teachers in subject-matter areas and the somewhat reduced teaching day reduces teacher desire to bring his or her class to the library or instructional center.

4. Large quantities of materials are useless to a teacher who needs a specific book, filmstrip, set of transparencies, or original teaching device within forty-eight hours or less. In addition, the material frequently arrives late, requires numerous forms or is in poor condition when it arrives. Requisitioning can be eliminated when materials are stored in individual classrooms.

5. The creative teacher and class may plan their work spontaneously, depending on immediate relevance. An unscheduled visit to the library would probably not be permitted or feasible within the usual structured schedules.

6. Unfortunately, many visits to the library fall short of classroom expectations.

Somewhere between the two positions of library (or instructional materials center) and the classroom library (or media corner) there exists a "happy media." Discussion of developing classrooms for maximum use of teaching media was the substance of chapter 2. Chapter 3 was concerned with the establishment of media centers. Media corners and media centers provide the stimulating appeals to the senses that can encourage a love of learning and develop patterns of inquiry. The guidelines listed earlier in this chapter offer a framework within which teachers, media specialists, administrators, and librarians can work together to improve both teaching and learning.

Moving the High School Classroom into the Library

The Educational Facilities Laboratories report asked and answered two obvious questions:

1. What do students do in school libraries?

    —Find answers to specific questions that arise either from the teaching process or from ordinary curiosity.

    —Go alone or as a member of a committee sent to get information.

    —Carry out study hall assignments; that is, spend a specific amount of time studying in the library.

    —Find material for projects such as a written report, a book review, a debate brief, or a research paper.

    —Learn how to use the keys of a library—card catalogs, bibliographies, reference books, periodical indexes, etc.

    —Look at motion-picture films, filmstrips, or other audiovisual materials. Study with a teaching machine, listen to phonograph records or tapes, listen and record voice for language study.

    —Locate quotations, excerpts, or data for speeches or projects.

    —Read just for the fun of reading—one book or a hundred.

    —Browse through current magazines and newspapers or look at the new book shelf.

    —Talk with other students.

    and

2. What do teachers do in school libraries? Activities similar to those mentioned for students, but they also

    —Confer with the library staff on relevent materials to use for class work: those appropriate for general presentation in the classroom, those most suitable for students working in small groups, and those appropriate for use on an individualized basis.

    —Preview films and filmstrips; confer on the purchase or rental of audiovisual materials, and on local production of same.

    —Consult with librarians [3] on book purchases, on the handling of special materials (pamphlets, sample magazines, government documents, etc.), on classification and cataloging problems, and on reader's problems and difficulties that the students may be having.[4]

These questions and their answers have taken on new dimensions because of the independent study programs that have moved strongly into high

---

[3] Teachers should also have opportunities to discuss resources and methods with other teachers.

[4] Ellsworth and Wagener, *The School Library*, p. 25.

schools across the country. Learning theorists and classroom teachers are more convinced than ever that learning is personal and must be "internalized." Self-instruction is consistent with student movements toward independent thought and the desire to be involved in decisions that affect their education.

The movement toward independent study began to appear in high schools as an organized plan for learning in the 1950s, and libraries designed after 1960 responded to this approach with study carrels, electronic equipment, media, and a variety of instructional materials and resources.

Photo 17. Students study high school courses in specially designed study carrels. (Photograph courtesy of West Hartford Public Schools, West Hartford, Connecticut; Robert L. Nay, Photographer.)

Libraries built before that time now probably require from two to four times the space and from five to ten times the number and variety of books and materials. Moreover, additional staffing is usually a requisite to the effective functioning of an instructional media center.

One of the many fine library facilities built in recent years is in Shawnee Mission South High School in Overland Park, Kansas. There is enough space in this facility to accommodate:

1. The greatest number of students likely to use it at peak period;
2. Books, media materials and media equipment needed for present pro-

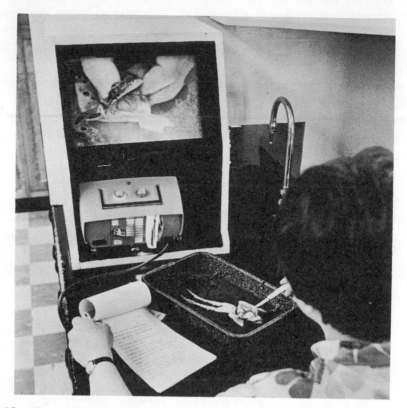

Photo 18. Students study high school courses in specially designed study carrels. (Photograph courtesy of State University College, Fredonia, New York; Terry S. Lindquist, Photographer.)

grams and, probably, programs of the distant future as well—yet the amount of space used solely for storage is minimal;

3. Student and teacher projects—fabrication of projectuals, slide sets, photo presentations, and other special work projects;

4. Efficient student research, without frustration and wasted motion.

This type of learning environment may foster group and independent research devoid of tension and inhibition caused by the lack of proper facilities. Well-designed facilities are essential if students are to elect and profit from independent study. Students who choose to work on their own are quickly "turned off" when they have to wait in line, sign numerous forms, travel from one section or floor to another in search of elusive items, and be informed that requested books and materials are under repair, misplaced, or not available.

Supermarkets are partially successful because of the superior market research undertaken to serve and please the consumer. Organization by category, visible signs, shelves within reach, attractive displays, and efficient check-out systems have all but driven the small grocery from the American scene.

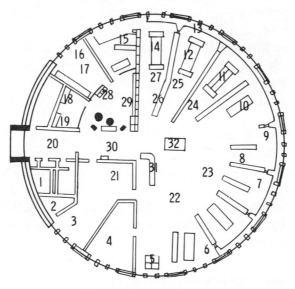

SHAWNEE MISSION SOUTH'S LIBRARY

1. Restrooms
2. Mechanical Equipment
3. Workroom
4. Professional Library
5. Carrels
6. Audiovisual Storage
7. Audiovisual Storage
8. General Reference Area
9. Stool
10. Individual Reading Table
11. Language Arts
12. Science
13. Audiovisual Storage
14. Social Science
15. Microfilm
16. Screen
17. Social Services
18. Study Carrels
19. Special Services
20. Entrance
21. Materials Preparation
22. Fine Arts Area
23. Technology Area
24. Study Carrel
25. Study Carrel
26. Book Shelves
27. Study Carrel
28. Paper Backs
29. Magazines
30. Card Catalog
31. Charging Desk
32. Display Unit

Figure 5–1. Shawnee Mission South High School, Overland Park, Kansas. Shaver & Company, Architects, Salina, Kansas. There is no storage room in Shawnee Mission South's library. All media materials are out in the open, conveniently grouped in subject matter areas.

Libraries must follow the same design in order to capitalize on independent study and self-motivation. In fact, automated supermarkets and libraries are discussed in the same paragraphs of writers who predict the future. Not only will cereals or soups, in the one case, and natural science materials, in the other, be stored centrally for rapid access and use, but pushbuttons or computers and electronic systems will render instant delivery of food supplies to waiting cars and information to students via television sets in the near future.

The Shawnee Mission High School library functions well for reasons other than merely easy-to-reach stacking by subject matter, however. Students are assigned to the library for a substantial portion of their academic schedule. One hour of every five or six in a given subject may be spent in the library.

In another realistic move, teachers and administrators recognized that few students are fully capable of truly effective "independent" study without some degree of professional guidance. Accordingly, the Shawnee Mission Library is staffed, as well as stacked and organized, for action. There is no clerical work for the librarians. The school employs clerks and secretaries to assist each of the three professionals, thus allowing them to perform three major roles as:

1. A library and administrative specialist for operations and library guidance on materials and procedures;
2. A media specialist for uses of equipment and needed arrangements; and
3. A learning-problem specialist for diagnosing problems and prescribing instructional solutions.

Honor students and teachers are assigned to the library to assist other students with in-depth work in subject matter fields.

Planning and Obtaining an Instant Library-Media Center: The Mobile Instructional Media Center (MIMC)

Mobile units have appeared in recent years as classrooms, planetariums, in-service vehicles, and, in at least one instance, as a rolling instructional media center with the express purpose of producing change. The change results from orientation and training of staff with subsequent planning of a local instructional media center when the Mobile Instructional Media Center (MIMC) leaves.

The following copy is taken directly from two brochures describing an ESEA Title III [5] project that has instituted change and brought the "media message" to several elementary schools in Nassau County, New York.

---

[5] Sponsored by the Board of Cooperative Educational Services (BOCES), Nassau County, New York and implemented by The Education Council (TEC), the research and development division of BOCES.

Planning Phase

mobile instructional media center
an esea title III pilot project

WHY MEDIA ?

The printed word is no longer the only means we have of communicating information and ideas, thoughts or feelings, in other words, of teaching and learning.
While educators recognize that reading is a vital part of education, they also
know that children learn by seeing and hearing as well as by reading and doing.
Knowing this, teachers often spend many hours developing files of pictures to
use in the classroom, or drawing pictures or diagrams on blackboards to illustrate an idea.

How much more convenient it would be if the pictures were available just a few steps away, in the school library. And how much better if not only pictures but other educational tools were also available there; the kinds of tools that help make an idea easier to understand, that make past events happen again today because they have been recreated on film, that bring a story or a poem to life, because it has been recorded by a fine actor. Modern technology has created these teaching tools, both the materials to be seen and heard and the machines that make seeing and hearing possible--records and record players, films and projectors, tapes and tape recorders. These are instructional media.

MEDIA ARE WHAT'S HAPPENING

Instructional media--films, filmstrips, records, tapes, transparencies, pictures--are as vital in schools today as textbooks and workbooks were yesterday. In the schools of tomorrow, libraries will provide these materials not only for teachers but also for children to use by themselves just as they now provide books. Before that tomorrow comes, however, we must catch up with today.

WHAT IS THE MOBILE INSTRUCTIONAL MEDIA CENTER?

Just as bookmobiles have brought library services to neighborhoods that did not have a public library building, so the MIMC has been designed to bring instructional media to school media centers. Its purpose is both to fill needs that have already been felt and to create a demand where none has yet occurred, so that media will become as natural a part of the educational scene as blackboard and chalk, and easier to find than pictures in a magazine.

The MIMC is a trailer full of ideas and materials for improving teaching and learning. It contains a variety of media and furnishes expert help in planning for their use. It provides preview facilities so that teachers can become familiar with what they are going to use before bringing it into the classroom. If a particular need is not met by the materials available, a graphics specialist will produce what is required. Groups of teacher-interns and new teachers can observe demonstration lessons using new media right on the trailer and learn how to use various kinds of equipment. This pilot will provide on-location, practical in-service training for elementary teachers and administrators. When the school administration and staff decide to create a permanent media center in its school building, the staff will assist in its design.

Pilot Operational Phase

MOBILE
INSTRUCTIONAL MEDIA CENTER
A VEHICLE FOR CHANGE

AN ESEA
TITLE III
PILOT
PROJECT

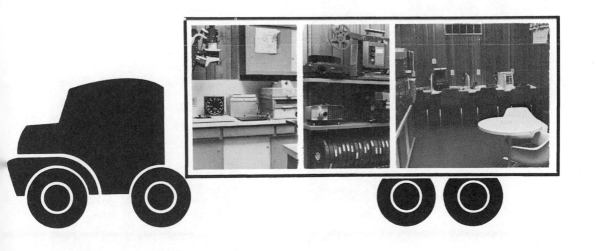

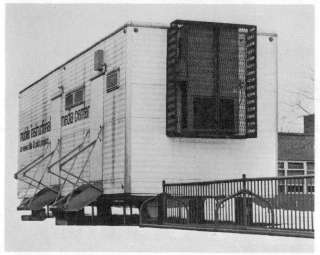

Developed as a supplement to the school library, the MIMC suggests that instructional
media belongs in the school library. Selection
and acquisition of all instructional materials
located in the MIMC, as well as the establishment of circulation and cataloging procedures,
were supervised and performed by school
librarians. Although the mobile unit is physically
separate from the school library, it is, in concept, inseparable from it.

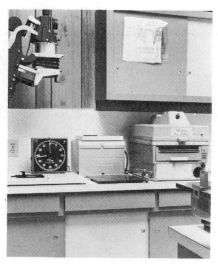

A graphics area has been equipped
with the latest and most versatile production facilities for the preparation of
special materials.

A large variety of instructional materials — 16mm films, 8mm film loops, study
prints, filmstrips, sound filmstrip sets,
tapes, records, and multimedia kits —
are located in the mobile unit for circulation within the school.

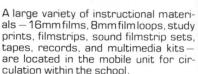

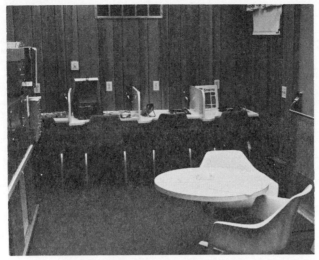

Before using these materials in the classroom, teachers may preview them at one of the four carrels provided in thc mobile unit.

An artist with training in graphics production designs special materials when commercial products are not available.

Assistance is provided to teachers by a media assistant in locating the right materials for a particular lesson or unit, and a complete library catalog of all materials also enables users to find what they need.

The elementary school IMC, to be not merely a storage place for books and other materials but the center for instructional media, requires of the people who staff it a wider and deeper acquaintance with varied means of communicating, both aural and visual. The librarian should be able to evaluate all media and recommend those best suited to a particular educational purpose. The clerical staff needs to develop skills in processing and distributing media efficiently and in preparing graphics materials.

Of paramount importance is the school administrator, who establishes a climate of acceptance by the faculty of the changed role of the library and its staff. An atmosphere conducive to experimentation, a willingness to change approaches and methods of instruction, and an easing of the IMC into its central role will be accomplished if the principal sets the pace with enthusiasm.

In this respect, the experience provided by the MIMC, even in the short time it has been operating, is instructive. Both staff members, the graphics technician and the media assistant, are engaged full time in meeting the needs of the school at which it is located. The organization of the MIMC required the substantial professional attention of a school librarian, with the cataloging assistance of another librarian. The active cooperation of the principal, his frequent encouragement of the teachers to visit the mobile unit and make use of its facilities, assured their enthusiastic acceptance and involvement. Teachers not only use the materials but evaluate them, suggest additional purchases, and support the project in every way.

As a result of this spirit, the school is planning a permanent IMC of its own, while the MIMC prepares to continue its innovative program in the next school it visits.

The instructional media center idea involves not only added physical facilities but is a dynamic concept for change within the school. The IMC is not simply a collection of instructional materials. It enhances the role of the school librarian, alters the function and use of the library, broadens the instructional program, increases teacher effectiveness and efficiency and results in improved learning.

THE CHANGING ROLE OF THE LIBRARIAN • The librarian is emerging as an instructional consultant in her areas of competence. She can provide knowledge and advice about books and other media to assist teachers in improving instruction.

The IMC, if used flexibly, will provide:
- For individual and small-group instruction
- For the scheduling of extra class visits
- Planning time to prepare bibliographies and resource lists for teachers
- Time for the librarian to maintain her familiarity with the media collection and with new materials as they are produced
- Time for planning and consultation with teachers on appropriate curriculum materials
- For planning and production of special materials

THE CHANGING ROLE OF THE TEACHER • As new instructional methods emerge, teachers have begun to recognize the need for incorporating more media into their classroom activities. The wish to do this, however, is often frustrated when instructional media are unavailable. This situation may be improved through the establishment of an IMC, a system for acquiring, organizing and circulating the materials that teachers need. When a variety of instructional materials are available teachers will employ them to the benefit of their classes' perception, understanding and education.

ADDITIONAL STAFF • An adequate para-professional staff to provide clerical and technical services is also required for:
- Handling of routine circulation procedures
- Typing and filing of catalog cards for all media
- Ordering and processing of instructional materials
- Typing of bibliographies, resource lists, etc.
- Using graphics equipment for the preparation of special materials

Ideally, two people should be assigned to perform clerical and graphics tasks: a library aide or clerk, and a graphics technician. As a realistic recommendation, at least one person with skills and training in typing, filing, and preparing graphics should be employed.

Incorporated in the design of the MIMC are rearview projection equipment and a moveable chalkboard as well as enough seating and space to provide facilities for group instruction, in-service training and demonstrations.

Suggested Changes in School

Present Library

Connecting Classroom

Suggested IMC

LIBRARIAN

GROUP

GRAPHICS

BOOKSHELVES

CARRELS

CARD CAT.

FILMS, TAPES

REAR-PROJECTED SCREEN

PROJ.

TEACHER AREA

EQUIP.

PAPERBACKS

ENTRY

Alternate Proposal • Where space is at a premium, as it is in many elementary schools, the "blueprint for action" includes alternate suggestions. Two relocatable classroom modules could be combined to form a single unit that will house both library and media facilities, providing additional space within the school (possibly where the library is located) and a complete media center that is easily accessible to pupils and staff.

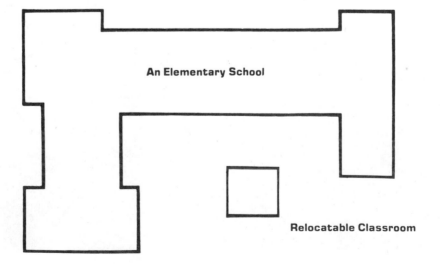

An Elementary School

Relocatable Classroom

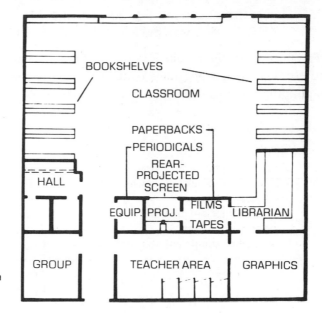

Relocatable Classroom

A Blueprint for Action • The MIMC, however, has not been designed as a permanent addition to the school. What is permanent is the concept it develops: that a full range of media services is vital for the best instructional program a school can provide for its pupils. Teachers, librarians, administrators, secretaries, and graphics specialists must be involved and trained in the MIMC to take full advantage of its potential. The Education Council provides a "blueprint for total involvement and action"—a complete plan for duplicating the media center within the school that has been served by the MIMC.

The service—the concept—the training—the blueprint—these are the sum of the contributions of the Mobile Instructional Media Center.

A CHECKLIST OF EQUIPMENT AND MATERIALS FOR AN
ELEMENTARY SCHOOL MEDIA PROGRAM

The purpose of the mobile instructional media center is to stimulate schools
to establish media programs of their own. Use this suggested checklist for
equipping a trailer—or an elementary school—in your district.

EQUIPMENT	INSTRUCTIONAL MATERIALS
Graphics	*Films*
Thermal copier—transparencies, both color and black and white, ditto masters	16mm
	8mm
	Filmstrips
Dry mount press—laminating, color lifting, dry mounting	Sound filmstrips
Photography equipment and supplies	Tapes
	Cassettes
	Records
	Transparencies
	Flat pictures
Audiovisual	*Supplies*
16mm projector	Graphics
8mm loop projector	Administrative
Super 8mm loop projector	Miscellaneous
Filmstrip projector	*Staff* (Ideal Team)
Record player	
Tape player	Graphics technician
Cassette player	Secretary
Slide projector	Librarian or media specialist
Storage	
Filmstrip cabinets	
8mm cartridge cabinets	
Tape cabinets	
Film shelving and racks	
Miscellaneous storage (sound filmstrip sets)	
Transparency and picture files	

The travels of the Mobile Instructional Media Center have excited some
teachers and principals to the extent that they have sent urgent letters re-
questing that the MIMC never be taken away! Bringing the "media moun-
tain" to "Mohammed school districts" in the form of a mobile IMC may be
the answer for motivating teachers, administrators and students to utilize media more extensively and, as a result, improve the teaching-learning process.

6

Planning Regional
Media Centers:
Functions and Facilities

Defining Media Center Functions: Regional Guidelines

Media center functions may be defined in several patterns. One would be operational like "There Ought to Be a Place," another would be categorical:

1. *Instructional Resources,* e.g., development and evaluation of slides, films, tapes, transparencies, and materials
2. *Equipment Resources,* e.g., projectors, television receivers, cameras
3. *Maintenance Services,* e.g., equipment, setups, repair, preventive maintenance
4. *Program Development,* e.g., video broadcasts, films, audio programs
5. *In-Service Development,* e.g., clinics, courses, individualized services
6. *Library Services,* e.g., film distribution, specialized filmstrips, audio and video tape deliveries
7. *Consultant Services,* e.g., building or media center designs, equipment and material selection

Still others utilize major media areas, e.g., television services, film services, administrative services, maintenance, graphics, and instructional materials.

Whichever pattern is used to describe media center functions, starting and running a comprehensive media program is, apparently, too comprehensive and costly a task for most districts. Furthermore, few administrators are trained to establish an outstanding media program. Fewer still are familiar with the logistics of *maintaining* a districtwide program—selecting and purchasing materials and then preparing and making the materials readily available to users. When the setting up of media centers is attempted under these conditions, chaos results in some districts—nothing at all results in others.

Photo 19. . . . maintaining a districtwide program—selecting and purchasing materials . . . (United States Air Force Academy Photo.)

The solution may be found in a growing trend toward regional, cooperative media centers.

—In California regional media centers have been operating through county offices for many years.

—In New York State "boards of cooperative educational services" (BOCES) operate regional media centers.

—In Michigan twenty-nine independent districts formed an intermediate district that was established in 1962 for the purpose of operating a media center.

—In Pennsylvania regional instructional materials centers (RIMC) have been functioning since the passage of the National Defense Education Act in 1958.

—In Massachusetts a cooperative film library has operated on a state-wide basis under the aegis of the department of education since the late 1940s.

Specific types of regional media centers will be able to solve many problems if the following guidelines are considered for planning and operation of the centers.

First, *the effect of any regional program must be felt, ultimately, in the classroom.* Teachers, students and regional center personnel should be able to point to evidence of direct service to every school building and its classrooms.

Second, *while regional centers may function as production centers and warehouses, they should be designed to serve staff members in individual schools.* Technicians must be available at the classroom level. Leadership and most warehousing should remain in the centers.

Third, *teachers should not be expected to function as technicians in or for the regional center.* They have important instructional tasks such as planning lessons and individualizing programs for students. The teacher should understand the processes of production; he should know how to work with media technicians and how to order materials. Aides should be available to do most of the technical work in all but the initial phases or in those instances when a teacher with technical ability and talent can translate a portion of an instructional task into media items.

Guideline one is critical, however. Once a regional media program has been initiated, every effort should be made to use the regional center as a means of bringing effective media into every classroom for the express purpose of improving teaching and learning. In this regard, good human relations principles of involvement, participation, communication, motivation, and individual need and fulfillment should be considered when utilizing *any* organizational guideline.

Designing Media Facilities: A Regional Solution

In 1963-64 co-author Jack Tanzman served as principal investigator for a U.S. Office of Education NDEA project to explore the role and feasibility of a regional educational media center. The results and advanced designs presented here will probably not be used *in toto* for many years to come, although the report has influenced many other projects—notably supplemental centers designed under ESEA Title III (see SCORE—A

Master Plan for Regional Services—this chapter) and some of the large learning center complexes in cities like Chicago.

A Regional Media Facility

The heart of a regional center must be research and curriculum development. Modern technology should be used to disseminate information and diffuse the results throughout the region via television, motion pictures, and distribution of published materials. Sophisticated facilities should be provided for the production of these materials.

Other services such as data processing, psychological and guidance counseling, demonstration classroom teaching, or closed-circuit television may be designed for any specific regional plan. Each of these must be planned and designed to meet the specific needs of a given regional center.

One usual service for the center is the distribution of instructional materials such as films, specialized and requested filmstrips, records, video tapes, etc. (The "media corner" and local media centers should house inexpensive and easily obtained materials.) Provision must be made for an instructional media center that would house any specialized materials produced by the regional center as well as commercial materials available for teacher education. If the production of projectuals and other media materials is contemplated, a production center—well-equipped and well-staffed—becomes essential.

To a large extent the design of a regional media facility will be determined by the services performed, by the number and type of districts involved and the location of the center. Nevertheless, certain criteria that are basic to any effective educational communications center can be set forth.

The regional center should be in a convenient location, near highways and within easy commuting distance of all of the participating districts. The building design and landscaping should be attractive, and the center should have dignity and appeal. There should be sufficient parking for large groups of teachers who may come to the center for special meetings.

Because the building would be used throughout the entire year, it should be completely air conditioned. Concerted effort should also be made to provide good lighting, ventilation and attractive interior decor. The use of carpeting should be seriously considered. It would also be sensible to build maximum flexibility into the interior since it is certain that the building's functions will be continually changing.

Obviously, a regional center can operate in temporary, rented or makeshift quarters, but to function best the center requires facilities designed to provide its specific services. In most cases these should be new structures. It is not necessary, however, to build the entire facility at one time. Those areas central to an active regional program should be completed in the first building stages, i.e., the professional library, conference spaces, an auditorium, and general administrative offices.

Some regions may not want specific curriculum specialists on their staff at all times, but space for research and curriculum people is essential. Space must also be provided for demonstration areas in which to exhibit materials and equipment while staff members are working on a project. An auditorium will make it possible to bring large groups of teachers together—an important objective of a regional organization.

Figures 6–1, 6–2 and 6–3 depict optimum plans for a building in which every conceivable service is offered in the best possible space. No effort is made to combine functions, no matter how logical such combinations might be. Thus, for example, there is room for a science materials distribution center, though this function could easily, and logically, be carried out through the instructional materials center, which is also included. On the other hand, the space designated for a science center might be used for humanities, foreign languages or physical education, if this becomes the desire of the participating districts.

Moreover, because the basic emphasis is to design a series of modules, each of which would be self-contained and each of which serves a specific function, no attempt is made to provide a final "functional" plan for this

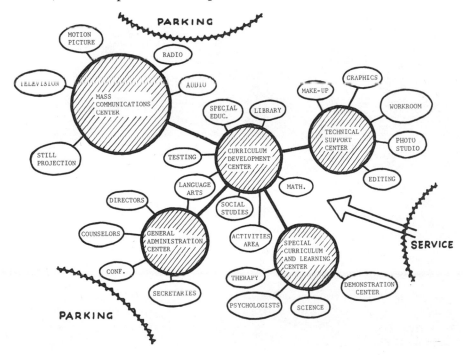

Figure 6–1. Designed by Shaver & Company, Architects, Salina, Kansas.

Figure 6–2. Designed by Shaver & Company, Architects, Salina, Kansas.

Figure 6–3. Designed by Shaver & Company, Architects, Salina, Kansas.

optimum center. Instead, each individual regional organization may examine these component modules and select those that might best serve a specific region.

The space within the building is organized into five centers: special curriculum and learning, curriculum development, technical support, mass communications, and general administration.

The centers are separated by function to permit efficient supervisory control. Traffic flow is important within each center as well as between the centers and throughout the structure. The architects must not only consider pedestrian traffic flow but must also analyze the traffic requirements for private automobiles and buses. It should be anticipated that there will be many student and faculty groups visiting the center and that these groups must be accommodated without impeding the program of the permanent staff stationed in the building itself.

REGIONAL EDUCATIONAL COMMUNICATIONS CENTER

The following specifications include all of the areas shown in Figure 6–3.

1. Total Building Area: 320,000 square feet.
2. Structural System: Reinforced concrete, Type 1 construction.
3. Mechanical System: Complete year-round air conditioning. Water, gas, compressed air and waste piping disbursed throughout building with flexible connections permitting the relocation of equipment requiring these connections.
4. Electrical: Underground network of wireways permitting electrical connections for any and all equipment and for relocating all equipment that requires electrical power.
5. Site: Minimum site requirement, 10 acres (unless a multistory structure is considered).
6. Estimated Cost: Costs would vary depending upon the location and construction of the center.

Space Program	*Gross Area*
Administration	25,000 sq. ft.
Regional Library and IMC	80,000 sq. ft.
Curriculum Development Center	75,000 sq. ft.
Radio and Television Studios	15,000 sq. ft.
Graphic Arts, Photo Studios, Printing	10,000 sq. ft.
Regional Museum and Art Gallery	30,000 sq. ft.
Auditorium	25,000 sq. ft.
Conference Center	10,000 sq. ft.
Science and Technology Center	40,000 sq. ft.

Service, Maintenance, Garage   10,000 sq. ft.

      Total   320,000 sq. ft.

The total area in the building is 320,000 square feet. The additional space not accounted for is in corridors, lobby, etc.

TV or Not TV? Regional Questions and Designs

While the fulfillment of television as an educational tool has not yet reached its maximum potential, few would be willing to say that television is not "here to stay." The technology to install educational television regionally and locally exists. Sufficient research exists to support its use as a successful educational tool.[1] The questions of "whether?" or "when?" are really dependent on fundamental sub-questions:

1. Which areas of curriculum weakness exist in the region to be served? Can educational television enhance those curriculum areas for students in the region? Would the cost for installing and operating educational TV exceed the cost of other programs designed to improve instruction in the region? Are existing "off-air" programs available? Do they, or could they, meet educational objectives?

Shortages of qualified and experienced teachers often exist in science, mathematics, art, and foreign language instruction at the elementary school level. At the high school level teachers and administrators frequently request (1) the extensive use of professionals and experts in subject matter fields, (2) persons skilled in observing and discussing current world and local situations, and (3) regional in-service training and the strengthening of subject departments where shortages of teachers exist, e.g., physics, Russian, Chinese, Afro-American studies.

2. Which type of television system or systems should be selected to meet the needs of each unique region?

There are five separate educational television systems available to an area. The selection should be determined largely by how the region intends to use ETV, the amount of money it has to spend through the pooling of resources and by the size and terrain of the region:

VHF Television.—The VHF (very high frequency) system is the kind most commercial channels use. Its primary use is for the region that wishes to reach the entire community—not just classrooms. With VHF equipment

---

[1] James W. Brown, Richard B. Lewis and Fred F. Harcleroad, *AV Instruction: Media and Methods* (3rd ed.; New York: McGraw-Hill Book Company, Inc., 1969), p. 303.

a regional center can blanket a town, a city or an area with instructional programs, documentaries about school activities, or even televised adult education courses. The equipment is relatively expensive and the system requires highly trained personnel. It necessitates operating a television station similar to the commercial stations that serve many small cities.

UHF.—Ultra-high-frequency television systems are similar to VHF stations. While UHF channels are available for school use at present, not all home sets are equipped to receive UHF telecasts. If you hope to reach the entire region, a survey is in order to see how many home TV sets in the region can receive UHF programs.

2,500-megahertz Transmission.—If the primary purpose is to televise to a cluster of schools (excluding private homes), then perhaps 2,500-megahertz transmission is the system to use. This system has worked very well in several districts. The operation consists of a low-cost, closed-circuit TV system that feeds the electronic signal into a special low-frequency transmitter. This system is far less expensive than UHF or VHF and requires less highly skilled technicians to operate. It has one great disadvantage: limited range.

Coaxial Cable (CATV).—A region can avoid the high cost of operating a transmitter—and still reach the schools in the area—by installing a coaxial cable system. In a coaxial cable operation, closed-circuit equipment is used to televise a program, but the signal is sent to receiving schools via a cable instead of being transmitted through the air. The result is an inexpensive way to reach regional schools—at practical ranges—with a clear TV signal that cannot be broken by outside interference. This system is especially valuable for districts located in hilly areas, since it does not require a straight line-of-sight between the transmitter and the receivers. Moreover, many commercial cable companies are offering free installation to schools as a community service.

Internal Closed Circuit.—Finally, the lowest-priced and most trouble-free system of all is the internal closed-circuit variety. Here the program originates in a studio within a school and is transmitted to various classrooms in the same building. The system is extremely limited, however, because it can serve only one building. Nevertheless, all new construction should include the installation of conduit (if not the wiring itself) to tie all teaching areas into a closed-circuit network. This built-in capability allows for many variations in the future—at greatly reduced expense.

3. How long will it take to install these systems?

Establishing a regional education system requires from sixteen to twenty-six weeks from bidding to completed installation, depending upon the system. For the internal closed-circuit and the coaxial cable units, buying, delivery and installation time should be minimal. The VHF, UHF, and 2,500-megahertz stations, however, include application to the Federal Communications Commission (FCC) for a broadcaster's license and construction permit and a request for permission to erect an antenna from the Federal Aviation Agency (FAA). The more complex the system the greater the amount of time required for installation and construction.

In general, there are six steps involved in establishing a complete educational television operation. First, the region has to complete a preliminary analysis of needs, decide on the equipment and accept bids. This should take from three to seven weeks. Then an application to the FAA and FCC for construction permits must be made. (Application to the FAA is needed only if an antenna is to be built on the roof.) The permit will be granted from five to six weeks later. The region can then "let" contracts and begin construction, which usually takes from two to three weeks. The final step, which is actual installation of the equipment, should require three to eight weeks.

4. Can a region obtain the staff needed for quality educational television?

School television programs should, when fiscally possible and educationally appropriate, have the type of quality appeal that draws millions of viewers (including school-age children) every evening and weekend. In any event, the staff at any regional or local level must be professional and talented.

A full-time director of the total program is the key. He must be experienced in educational television (ETV), not just commercial TV, and must be able to train others in their jobs as well as oversee the entire operation. Likely places to get help in recruiting a director are colleges and universities with programs in ETV, the National Center for School and College Television, the National Association of Educational Broadcasters (NAEB), the NEA's Department of Educational Technology (DAVI), and the newly developed University Consortium in Educational Media and Technology (UCEMET).[2]

A staff is also needed to operate equipment, man the cameras, set lighting properly, and monitor, tape, and broadcast programs. A technician is also vital to a smoothly functioning operation.

Maintenance of equipment can be critical, and depending on the scope of the projected regional program, additional skilled maintenance technicians should be employed, or the work should be contracted to professional maintenance firms.

---

[2] Indiana University, Michigan State University, the Oregon State System of Higher Education, Syracuse University, and the University of Southern California.

As for the content of TV programs, many systems employ program and teacher-coordinators. These would have to be fully trained in television techniques. A number of colleges offer such training courses today.

Other teachers are needed to prepare and present programs. They must know their subject matter thoroughly and must be given training in television techniques. They can be either full- or part-time TV teachers. One scheduling device might be to have teachers develop and tape their TV presentations during the summer, leaving them relatively free for regular classroom work during the school year.

Art work and secretarial work also must be provided to create displays and type scripts.

There are two schools of thought concerning the time, effort and money expended to prepare "quality" tapes and programs. The first maintains that the same kind of care and elaborate use of movie studio procedures for rehearsals and repeated "takes" of scenes should be employed for ETV. This group believes that the slow progress of ETV is caused by inferior technical quality, indifferent scripts, and mediocre performances and direction to which students respond very poorly. The second school believes that even if cost were not a factor (and it is), certain programs and presentations do not require elaborate staging, rehearsals, professional actors, and numerous takes. They argue that spontaneity, realism and low-budget creativity are all that is necessary to stimulate and motivate students.

We believe that both groups present valid arguments and both points of view have merit. The truth is that educational television today takes neither road. Insufficient funds, inadequately trained personnel and a lack of realism and creativity result in less than adequate ETV. Decisions should be made concerning the relative importance of types of lessons, reasons for staging, multiple uses of tapes, and other instructional objectives before money is expended, or *not* expended, for a particular program.

5. What are the design elements of a county or regional educational television center?

A. Direct electronic linkage to and from existing state and interstate television networks, which in turn will link aural-visual information centers of a regional, state and national structure
   1) Clearinghouse for televised communications transmitted into and out of the county
   2) Storage center for desired instructional information including tapes and films that come from sources outside the county
   3) Storage center for tape and film resources belonging to schools and made available for exchange
B. Evaluation

      1) Material screened for general quality

      2) Recommendations made to potential users

      3) User groups evaluate and decide either to store for use or discard

C. Production of television materials not available from other sources

      1) Studio facility is in the center

      2) Mobile television production facility for outside and remote location production

      3) Contracts with other production facilities

      4) Facilities and staff to duplicate and disseminate guide materials and catalogs for all programing material

D. Computer system

      1) Storage and retrieval via television of data displayable in alpha-numeric format

         a) Educational research statistics

         b) General educational statistics

         c) General records of required types

      2) Computerization of evaluations and use of recommendations for aural-visual materials in storage

      3) Computerized scheduling of transmission of information from the center to the subcenters

E. Transmission of information from the center to users

(Note: All transmission systems should be color capable.)

      1) Methods used by the center

         a) Point-to-point interconnection from center to each of four subregional instructional television fixed service centers

         b) Point-to-point interconnection with county studios

         c) Point-to-point interconnection with cable TV (CATV) terminal

         d) Point-to-point transmission with colleges and universities

      2) Functions served by the center

         a) Instructional tapes and films are evaluated

         b) Programing samples are "market tested" by use in simulation of instructional setting in which materials are intended for use

         c) Materials are validated or invalidated by test and measurement

         d) Recommendations for use are transmitted to computer base at center

F. Functions of subregional transmission centers

      1) Retrieve materials from center, store temporarily and retransmit to requesting schools in their quadrants according to schedule demands (school buildings may elect to adjust their own schedules via their own video recorders)

2) Maintain local production facility and minimum staff required for limited production of materials so localized that the center should not produce them

G. Field services
1) Workshop team with portable demonstration units to assist teachers in utilization of general and specific television programing
2) School facilities team consisting of engineer and assistants to assist in developing plans and specifications for desired local school television facilities
3) Maintenance team on call to all schools in county
   a) Receiver repair
   b) Distribution system repair
   c) Video recorder repair
   d) Emergency replacement equipment

6. Which instructional functions should be served by a regional television center?

The partial failures, slow development and lukewarm "reception" of educational television are often caused by the inability to mesh transmission and school schedules. In addition, inferior or mediocre instructional lessons, irrelevant programing, lack of training or preparation of "receiving" teachers, inadequate funds, facilities or personnel, poor orientation of taxpayers and educators, and reliance on outdated teaching techniques can all be contributing factors. Some of these problems can be overcome by the suggestions provided above. Others can be solved by employing public relations techniques to convey the idea of effective usage, e.g., demonstration tapes, training teams, workshops, speakers' bureaus, broadcasts, and news stories.

Of importance for success is the consideration of a rationale for broadcasting service that is based on current individual school needs and that avoids past mistakes, such as the transmission of lessons during class time which may be inferior to local teacher presentations for a variety of reasons.

Consideration, then, should be given to regional programing that meets local needs, fills in gaps, adds creativity, and provides instructional services not met in any other way:

1. Live and video taped news of the region
2. Live and video taped news of the state, the nation and the world
3. Selected pre-kindergarten through post-college graduate programing based on needs, requests and collaborative design by the agencies concerned
4. Adult and cultural programing

5. College and university courses
6. In-service courses and "specials"
7. Vocational and job training programing
8. County and regional services and government information programing
9. Programing for the disadvantaged
10. Programing for the handicapped and ill

In every case, storage and delayed transmission, before and after school time programing, and independent retrieval should be considered to assist educational television to mature as an instrument of instruction.

Cable TV (CATV): The Link to the Future

Cable TV, briefly described under coaxial cable earlier in this chapter, merits special consideration as a potential link to the future. Its advantages offer opportunities for teaching and learning that are only beginning to be tapped.

Advantages

1. Low cost—subscribers pay monthly fees
2. There is unimpeded transmission to areas formerly blacked out by terrain or distance
3. Clear pictures—signals picked up by the antenna are amplified in the control room at the base of the tower and are relayed to sets in the system at full strength, which is especially important for color TV in urban centers with tall buildings
4. Multiple channels—12, 21 or more will be available for special programs and services

Implications

1. Free installations in schools by franchise-seeking companies will speed television linkage among schools, universities, county agencies, industry, the region, and state and national networks.
2. Costs for purchase and operation of expensive transmission equipment will be eliminated and encourage the use of ETV.
3. Clear signals will enhance the appeal of instructional programs and special programs with educational substance.
4. Multiple channels and links will simulate learning environments in the home or neighborhood learning centers. Programs for small groups may be scheduled as well as more universally broadcast presentations.
5. Cables will permit eventual development of retrieval systems for in-

dividualized reception and study of computer programs, video tapes, films and reference material. Two-way communication and video recording is also within the realm of the possible, if not immediately feasible.

6. Special programs of local interest, e.g., person-to-person dialogues, debates on bond issues, community projects, tele-printed news, local problem solving, sports events, county demonstrations, cultural "cablecasts" for disadvantaged and student forums can be developed for each community or region.

Cable TV has the potential to link people and their communities to improve their future through relevant and immediate broadcasting with educational implications.

SCORE: A Master Plan for Regional Services

Among the several regional centers for cooperative educational services now being planned or developed throughout the United States, one of the more ambitious and far-reaching is the educational cooperative proposed for Nassau County, Long Island, New York.

Called SCORE—an acronym for Supplementary Centers for Organizing Regional Education—the project has grown, in part, out of an original feasibility study sponsored by the Office of Education in July, 1963. (See "Designing Media Center Facilities: A Regional Solution," this chapter.) The study investigated the feasibility and role of a regional educational communications center and determined ways in which, through cooperation, schools could provide special educational facilities and programs beyond the reach of any individual school or school district. The study concluded that such regional centers were not only feasible and desirable for improving the educational resources available to the schools in a region but were also adaptable for cooperation with nonschool groups, could be used as work-study or manpower retraining centers, and could be used for the special training of teachers.

Administrators and educators in Nassau County were quick to note the potential value of a regional center for the area. A 298-square-mile region of Long Island, bordered by New York City on the west and Suffolk County on the east, Nassau County had been experiencing a dramatic population growth since World War II. This growth had not been planned, and numerous communities have grown up, forming an intricate and often overlapping pattern of independent townships, incorporated villages, school districts and trading areas. Though the county is a distinct economic and social region, it lacks a central population center. Its population of 1,400,000 persons is spread throughout the county in 133 separate communities. The student population is served by 56 legally autonomous public school districts and over one hundred nonpublic elementary and secondary institutions. Obviously, a regional center could offer important capabilities for extended educational services beyond the reach of any of these individual schools.

Nassau County was fortunate in that it possessed considerable past experience in inter-district cooperation. Patterns of cooperation and channels of communication already existed. Equally important was the fairly widespread recognition on the part of county administrators and educators of the need for expanded services if Nassau County were to continue to provide the best education possible for all its residents.

Initiative was taken by the Nassau County Association of Chief School Administrators. One school district, acting on behalf of 56 other Nassau County school districts, applied for a planning grant under Title III of ESEA. It was granted, and early in 1966 the planning program began. Direction and governance were made the function of the Federal Programs Committee appointed by and from the Nassau County Association of Chief School Administrators. THE EDUCATION COUNCIL for School Research and Development was established as the agency of contract for executing planning activities. A major objective of the project was the establishment of a master network design of supplemental educational services.

Initial planning focused immediately upon defining both the needs and the resources, educational and cultural, of Nassau County. Project planners were determined to involve all county educational and cultural institutions in the program, and all were contacted for an assessment of both their needs and their resources. Liaison was established with the New York State Education Department and with, between and among representatives of business, industry and institutions of higher learning in the county. School administrators, teachers, and supervisors were all surveyed for their views on what services they felt were most needed. Visits were made to exemplary and innovative organizations and programs around the nation for a firsthand understanding of what had been and was being done. The thoroughness with which the program was planned is one of its outstanding features; when the final report was submitted, it was a detailed analysis of the educational and cultural needs of the county's entire preschool to adult population, with step-by-step recommendations for implementing the projected program.

Basically, SCORE calls for a regional center and at least four supplemental centers serving the entire county. The regional center, responsible for continually assessing the educational and cultural needs of the county, will determine priorities on an individual school district basis and conduct long-range planning for continued improvement and development of services. This regional center began operations in February, 1969, when the SCORE ESEA Title III Center moved into new quarters containing 36,000 square feet of floor space under the legal auspices of the Board of Cooperative Educational Services (BOCES) in Nassau County. The merger with BOCES was a major step in carrying forward the vision of SCORE because BOCES is based on an act of the New York State legislature and has been a major factor in developing cooperative services throughout the state for the past decade. Further, it will be able to continue the operation of government projects when they cease to be federally funded, at a minimum cost to the participating schools. This fiscal advantage has proved of immediate value since federal funds phased out in 1969 on two Nassau County ESEA Title III projects, the South Oyster Bay Supplementary Education Center and the Outdoor Education and Conservation Education Project. Both of these projects will be continued despite the cessation of federal funding.

In brief, the regional center is viewed as a catalyst for innovation and change, a central office initiating and coordinating special projects and, eventually, disseminating the results of these projects to the entire county as workable programs within the context of the long-range plan for the region. Special research and development projects will be passed on to the supplemental centers for implementation at the district and individual school level.

Initial planning for the regional program focused on nine specific areas: (1) curriculum development and adaptation, (2) social studies planning and services, (3) in-service training, (4) pupil-personnel services, (5) instructional media, (6) library services, (7) cultural services, (8) science services, and (9) data automation. Recommendations were submitted to the regional center for programs needed and possible in each of these areas. Studies were conducted by cooperating school districts, subject specialists and consultants from universities and industry.

On the basis of these studies and the findings of the earlier feasibility study, Nassau County's Title III regional program recommended initial incorporation of four of twelve proposed modules—curriculum, in-service, television, and instructional materials—as examples of specific operational tasks. The curriculum module will modify courses so they are especially suited to the mass media and develop curriculum for such programs as Title I, manpower development and training and areas of specific need, e.g., prevention of narcotics addiction, health education and family living, and social studies discovery units (Afro-American history, geography, pollution and other critical issues of the day). The instructional materials module will gather and design the necessary materials for the courses. The television module will draw heavily upon both the curriculum and instructional materials modules.

These modules have been incorporated into the regional center. The building will be essentially administrative in function and will house the general staff, including vocational and special education, research and development, the business office, a computer center, a professional library for teachers and administrators, a bureau of publications, TV production facilities, in-service facilities, curriculum development work areas, a warehouse for instructional materials, and a graphics center.

The remaining facilities and programs envisioned in the regional plan will be developed on a priority basis as funds and time permit.

Figures 6–4 through 6–8 illustrate the range of one county's plans for a regional and supplemental centers. When fully operational, the regional

THE PROPOSAL -
A) A REGIONAL CENTER including conference center, science & tech. center, administration, curriculum development, lab. school, regional library & IMC, ETU, etc.
B) FOUR SUPPLEMENTAL CENTERS including cultural center, administration, in-service training, area library & IMC, field house - exhibit center, and a special educational facility at each.

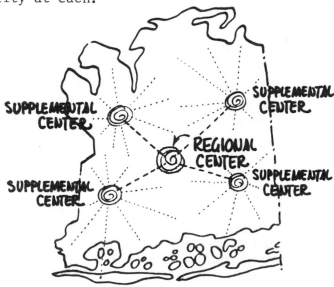

Figure 6–4. Designed by Charles W. Brubaker, Partner, The Perkins and Will Partnership, Architects, Chicago, New York and Washington.

THE REGIONAL CENTER

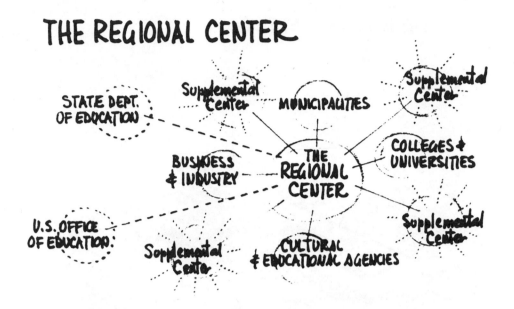

SPACE PROGRAM	GROSS AREA
Administration & coordination of resources & services to supplemental centers, to individual school districts, municipalities, business, universities, cultural agencies ... offices, data processing, services, etc.	$ 25,000
Regional library and Instructional Materials Center incl. admin, purchasing, storage, repair, distribution, etc.	80,000
Curriculum development, in-service training, demonstration facilities, and laboratory school	75,000
Radio and Television studios	15,000
Graphic arts & photo studios, printing shops,etc.	10,000
Regional museum and art gallery	30,000
Auditorium	25,000
Conference center, incl. cafeteria & dining	10,000
Science & technology center	40,000
Service, maintenance, garage, etc.	10,000
TOTAL	$320,000

Figure 6–5. Designed by Charles W. Brubaker, Partner, The Perkins and Will Partnership, Architects, Chicago, New York and Washington.

THE REGIONAL CENTER

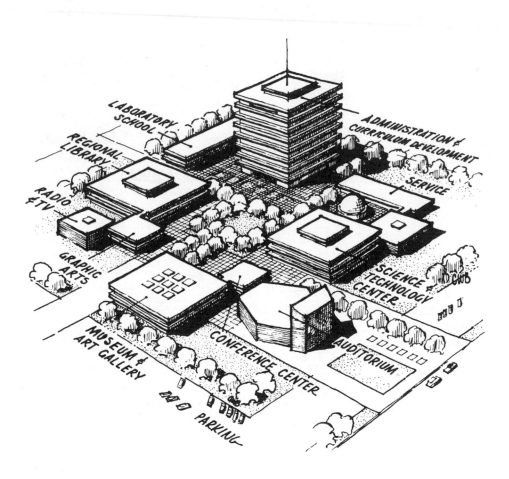

Figure 6–6. Designed by Charles W. Brubaker, Partner, The Perkins and Will Partnership, Architects, Chicago, New York and Washington.

A SUPPLEMENTAL CENTER

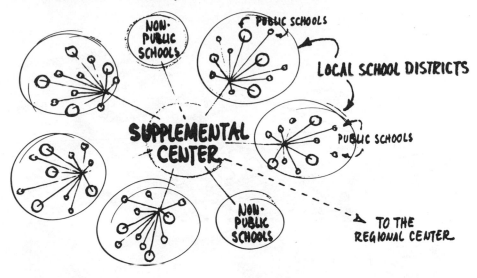

SPACE PROGRAM	GROSS AREA
Administration & coordination of resources & services to local school districts, to individual schools, and to individual teachers, students, & adults ... offices, conf., work, data processing, services, etc.	$ 15,000
Supplemental library and Instructional Materials Center	15,000
In-service training facility	5,000
Cultural center:	
Music Hall seating 2000	40,000
Workshop theater .. flexible space	5,000
Recital Hall seating 250, plus music facilities	5,000
Gallery-foyer-lounge serving 3 above assembly places	5,000
Art studios, craft shops, etc.	10,000
Field House-sports arena-phys. ed. & exhibition center	40,000
Special educational facilities-labs, shops, classrooms, etc. for advanced work (different emphasis at each center)	40,000
TOTAL	$180,000

Figure 6-7. Designed by Charles W. Brubaker, Partner, The Perkins and Will Partnership, Architects, Chicago, New York and Washington.

A SUPPLEMENTAL CENTER

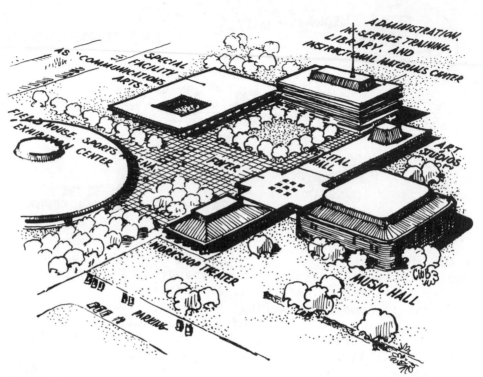

Figure 6–8. Designed by Charles W. Brubaker, Partner, The Perkins and Will Partnership, Architects, Chicago, New York and Washington.

center will extend educational and cultural opportunities for all county residents through a broad spectrum of supplemental services. The plans may seem visionary, but perhaps this is one shape of the future. All of the elements described exist in regions across the country. Perhaps you, as a reader, can aid in establishing such needed services in your region—even better! [3]

---

[3] For readers interested in learning more about Nassau County's vision of change, a motion picture is available from The Education Council, 125 Jericho Turnpike, Jericho, New York 11753. Entitled *Score For Tomorrow*, the film explains a cooperative approach to the problems of the American educational system, nationwide, and depicts the urgency for change through the pooling of resources. Twenty-nine minutes, 16mm, color, the film is offered at the nonprofit cost of $145.

7

Using Technology Wisely
to Serve Students:
Principles for
Administrators and Teachers

How to Build Around New Teaching and Learning Ideas

There are few knowledgeable citizens who will still maintain that if you had a good teacher such as "Mark Hopkins on the end of a log and a student at the other end" infinite learning could take place. Understanding of learning, the explosion of knowledge, the high degree of specialization, and the almost unbelievable advances of technology render obsolete the log (or log cabin, as the quote should read) as an effective teaching and learning space.

Despite increased awareness of the value of dynamic and flexible space that can embrace team teaching, multimedia instruction, independent study, and other newer instructional procedures, schoolmen and architects continue to design schools in box-like patterns that date back to the 1840s. There are notable exceptions, of course, and Riverview Gardens, Missouri, is one of these. That district completed two almost identical elementary school buildings in 1963 with spaces designed to provide the latest teaching techniques for all students.

In general, the shape of a school should be dictated by instructional ideas and curriculum needs. Beauty and economy do not have to be sacrificed—

Photo 20. Building around new teaching and learning ideas. (Photograph courtesy of Shaver and Company, Architects, Salina, Kansas.)

Photo 21. Beauty and economy do not have to be sacrificed. (Photograph courtesy of Shaver and Company, Architects, Salina, Kansas.)

they usually mesh with functional design. The following details and cuts of the district's Valley Winds and Lewis and Clark elementary schools indicate the many facilities—and most of the equipment—necessary to give the district the most modern elementary school program in the nation.

The functional beauty of the buildings lies very largely in the planning that went into them. Each school was constructed to meet a specific educational philosophy and program. At the same time, the district's planners (assisted by Dr. John W. Gilliland of the Tennessee University School Planning Laboratory), designed facilities that could be used even if the district decided to retain the most conventional teaching methods.

Designed by architect John Shaver, each building might be described generally as a snail-shaped school (see Figure 7–1). The central whorl of

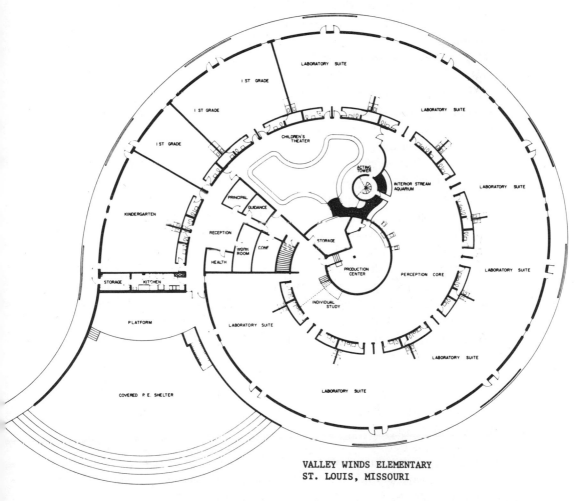

VALLEY WINDS ELEMENTARY
ST. LOUIS, MISSOURI

Figure 7–1. Valley Winds Elementary, St. Louis, Missouri. Designed by Shaver & Company, Architects, Salina, Kansas.

the "snail" houses a resource center (essentially an enhanced library), an area for individual or small-group instruction, a theater that will double as an area for large-group instruction, and administrative offices. Except for the offices and theater, this entire area is actually one large, open space subdivided by furniture.

The outer whorl contains a circle of classrooms carpeted for acoustical privacy and opening onto the central whorl. The walls between the classrooms are constructed of a light material that can be removed easily if that change proves desirable. (The rooms had been planned originally with movable walls, but these were eliminated as an economy measure.) At the point that is best described as that area where the snail comes out of his shell, there is a covered area for physical education.

Finally, at the core—the "heart" of the school in more ways than one—is a planning and work area from which the staff obtains its materials and equipment.

The classrooms are equipped with several instructional devices. For example, there are "instant chalkboards," four-foot sections of wallpaper-type material that will adhere to any vertical surface. The wall in the "front" of the room is several feet higher than the rear, in keeping with the principles of good projection. There is an abundance of display space (flannel, tack, and bulletin boards).

A unique feature planned for the future is the "nerve center," operable only by the teacher, that will become the key to the educational atmosphere of the classroom. In addition to controlling such ordinary utilities as lights and temperature, the nerve center will have direct connections to a "bank" of previously taped lessons. By dialing keyed numbers, a teacher can draw these lessons from the bank and present them to the class through a large speaker, or to individual students through earphones and electrical terminals around the periphery of the room. The nerve center will also have connections for television viewing, and provisions for two-way voice communications with the bank or other locations such as the principal's office.

The resource center (library), has space equivalent to about seven conventional classrooms. In close conjunction with the individual study and small-group instruction area, this section is critical in the development of new ideas for learning.

Separately or together (a portable wall is used) these spaces can be arranged in a variety of seminar or discussion areas as required. Most of the furniture is portable. The area is acoustically treated with carpeting and other sound-controlling devices. Individual study booths are wired and always available for students doing research or making up missed lessons; all have access to stored materials directly from the bank.

RIVERVIEW GARDENS SCHOOL

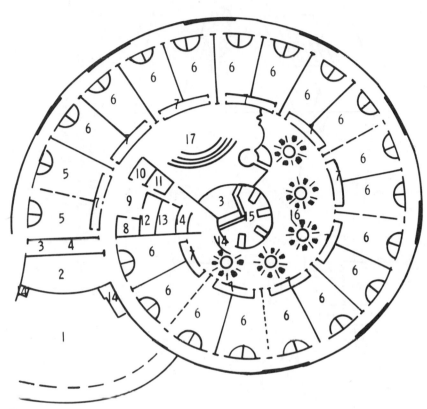

KEY

1. Limited Shelter	7. Restroom + Storage	13. Conference
2. Stage	8. Health	14. Stairs
3. Storage	9. Reception	15. Teacher's Work Area
4. Kitchen	10. Principal	16. Resources, Ind. Study
5. Kindergarten	11. Guidance	17. Children's Theater
6. Classroom	12. Workroom	

Figure 7–2. The snail shape of Riverview Gardens School cut costs by reducing corridors to absolute minimum; it provides easy access to large- and small-group areas for all students and to work area for all teachers. Designed by Shaver & Company, Architects, Salina, Kansas.

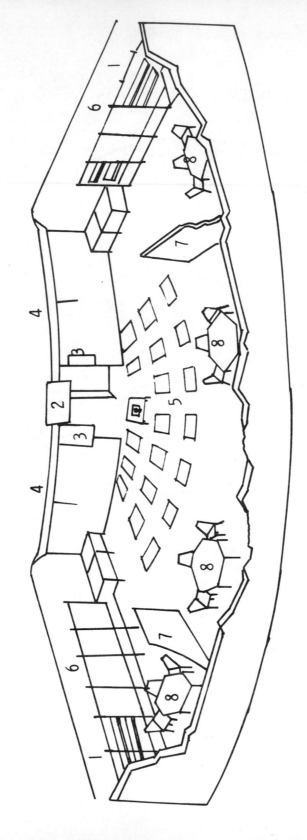

Figure 7-3. A double classroom provides these facilities: (1) a carrel for individual study; (2) a projection screen; (3) a projected "nerve center"; (4) instant chalk surface; (5) space for large-group instruction; (6) modular wall components; (7) space dividers; and (8) tables for small-group instruction.

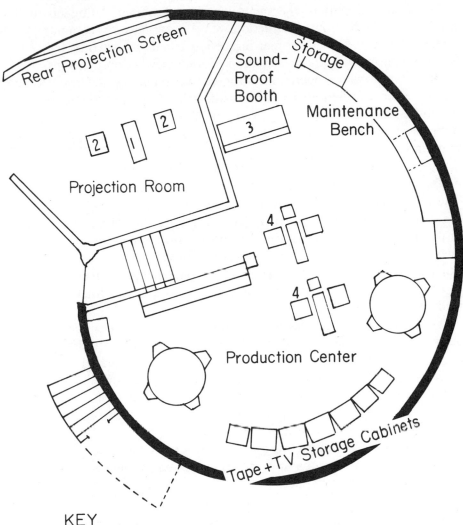

KEY
1. Remote-controlled movie projector
2. Slide projectors
3. Magnetic tape library control console
4. TV Camera, Multiplexer, and projectors

Figure 7–4. This two-story section of the building houses teacher work areas on its mezzanine floor.

The entire resource center has a versatile conduit system that will provide for any future expansion or innovation.

The theater is part of the same complex. Accommodating up to 300 children for large-group instruction, stage programs or community activities, it is equipped with rear-projection capability so that lights may be left on during a media presentation with no viewing obstructions.

Basic to the whole operation is the central planning and resource materials center. Located at the heart of the school, it will also be central to the entire program. Here a technician and teachers' aides prepare materials for projection, teachers record lessons for future use, and equipment and materials are stored.

The convenient location of the preparation area provides easy access to all the resources of the "library," the administrative center, and the theater. The area is back-to-back with the theater and has a direct connection to the stage. It contains the rear-projection equipment with a duplicate set of controls. The preparation area also houses the stored tape programs and television equipment as well as several key pieces of auxiliary equipment. For example, the district has acquired equipment that enables technicians to convert original materials into projectuals, with copies for teachers and students.

All of the media facilities were designed to school needs specifications. Surprisingly, the final cost of the building was slightly less than the cost of a conventional structure. The architect's design eliminated all corridor space—space that costs money to build, but which contributes nothing to the learning process. The space in this building was designed for learning. Most youngsters will probably learn far more seated on carpets with their peers than on the end of a log—"wooden" you?

If reductions in building costs are not sufficient to duplicate Valley Winds in your district, employ the approaches suggested in chapters 2 and 3, to develop better learning spaces.

Media Equipment and Materials: Strengths and Weaknesses

A list of basic equipment—their cost, and types of general use—was described in chapter 2. The chart that follows outlines the characteristic strengths and weaknesses of media equipment and materials from the teacher's point of view.

OVERHEAD PROJECTOR AND TRANSPARENCIES

Strengths	Weaknesses
1. Simplicity of operation.	1. Possible reliance on overhead to

Strengths	*Weaknesses*
2. Teacher faces class and controls the teaching process.	camouflage overused lecture methods.
3. Generates instant rapport with group—*large* or *small*.	2. Time-consuming effort may be spent on creation of suitable transparencies—often with dubious results.
4. Especially effective for large-group presentations.	
5. May be used with external light control, permitting seat work, notetaking, etc.	3. Cost of good commercially prepared transparencies may seem high for local budget.
6. Overlays permit timed and sequenced instruction.	4. Durability may prevent updating based on new knowledge or changes in equipment and/or materials.
7. Large, bright and colorful image; appeals to the visual sense.	
8. Teacher or student may write on or point to transparency.	
9. Immediate appearance of teacher's additions.	
10. Teachers and students may create own work; chalkboard presentations need not be duplicated endlessly.	
11. Special effects—disclosure, bright color, motion with polarized light, and multiple images with sound—are possible.	
12. The availability of increasing number of high quality commercial transparencies with guides.	
13. Durability.	
14. Ease of preparation of appropriate material on local basis.	
15. Flexibility.	

RECORD PLAYERS AND RECORDS

1. Simplicity of operation.	1. Visually oriented students may not respond to recordings alone.
2. Choice of group or individual listening; appeals to the auditory sense.	2. Lack of developed teaching techniques with sound recordings.
3. Availability of high quality commercial materials, professional renditions, actual events.	3. Lack of developed listening skills by students.
4. Moderate cost of recordings.	4. Danger of poor quality reproduction through use of inferior or worn-out equipment.
5. Relative durability.	

FILMSTRIP PREVIEWS AND FILMSTRIPS

1. Provides independent study and work.	1. Requires considerable time for checking, appraisal and guidance

Strengths	*Weaknesses*
2. Can be programed for continuous learning at the student's rate of growth and interest.	for an individual student.
3. A large quantity of commercial filmstrips are available.	2. Requires considerable time and training for selecting appropriate and high quality filmstrip sequences.
4. Relative low cost and high durability.	3. Fixed sequencing is unavoidable as compared to transparency or 2×2 slide use.
5. Ease of operation.	
6. Do not require room darkening.	
7. Important to "multimedia" use for follow-up, in-depth study, etc.	

FILMSTRIP PROJECTOR AND FILMSTRIPS

1. Relative low cost for projector and filmstrips with or without sound.	1. In some instances still photographs are not as effective as motion pictures.
2. Useful means of illustrating concepts and adding meaning to words.	2. May be used to disguise overused lecture methods.
3. Can be effective for teaching factual information.	3. Mediocre or poorly developed filmstrips that lack detail, clarity or well-developed sequences may inhibit learning.
4. Suited to individualized instruction or group participation.	
5. May be used for a variety of teaching purposes: to help teach skills, to understand symbols, to teach information, to review learnings, to build aesthetic appreciation, to generate group interest, focus and participation through discussion and student-prepared visuals and recordings.	
6. Lesson paced to teacher's needs.	
7. Encourages student use with or without class involvement.	

TAPE RECORDER AND RECORDINGS

1. Takes advantage of student's curiosity and natural interest in hearing themselves.	1. Requires some training and experience.
2. Can motivate students to improve their speech and presentations, and to do creative work.	2. Students generally respond better to multimedia presentations.
3. Can encourage self-evaluation and peer or teacher evaluation involving performance and growth, in a variety of activities, e.g., oral reading, discussing, debating, speaking, pronunciation and usage in foreign languages.	3. Requires annotations, indexing, careful filing, some maintenance and care.
	4. Can become recreation rather than re-creation.
	5. Danger of poor quality reproduction through use of inferior or worn-out equipment.

Strengths

4. Assists in individualizing instruction; can be programed; teachers can join listening groups or monitor a variety of learning activities that can be designed and assigned for individual students or groups of students.
5. Are particularly useful in rearrangement and editing of materials or alterations in sounds (speed, tone, etc.) for individuals or group lessons.
6. Permits delayed use: completion of missed assignments, use in future projects, analyses with new perspectives.
7. Can facilitate patterns of repetition, rhythm, or scrambled material, depending upon a teacher's lesson design.
8. Relative simplicity of operation, low cost and ease of duplication and transportation.
9. Can be perfected for quality through deletions, alterations, re-recording, etc.
10. Permits synchronization with pictures, exact timing of sequences, use of pre-selected portions, interviews, creative homework, etc.
11. Allows instant recording and storage of noteworthy events, unusual activities, etc.
12. Possibility of "tape" pals as well as "pen" pals internationally.

Weaknesses

6. Possibility of inadvertent loss of program (accidental erasure) not present with records.

8 AND 16MM FILM PROJECTOR AND FILMS

1. Combines visual motion with sound, which can contribute to effective teaching and learning.
2. Can provide common experiences for groups.
3. Can be used for testing, motivation, problem solving, creative responses and new activities, information, reacting, writing, and to stimulate student film making.

1. Can be used to "kill time" instead of using film time to learn.
2. Requires considerable teacher preparation and training to preview, create lessons, build specific expectations, orient class or group to importance, show film and follow up with other appropriate teaching and evaluative exercises.

Strengths	*Weaknesses*
4. Aids in depicting history, or important events. Combined sight and sound with appropriate emotional tone can aid students in identifying, understanding and, in a sense, to be "there."	3. Requires study guides, in-service training for proper use, pre-testing and post-testing for effective results, reshowings.
5. May motivate and provide understandings when other methods such as discussing, reading, explaining, etc., fail; color, drama, clarity, and sequencing can aid the learning process.	4. Can be overdone in point of view of "massed" films in series at regular intervals—"a schedule" without attention to the learning process.
6. Can provide relevance by powerful depiction of life as it is with continuity of action that is difficult to duplicate with other media.	5. Can tend to exclude active participation by the "spectators"—requires teacher planning and ingenuity in stopping film, repeating, following up with relevant and real activities.
7. Overcomes physical and logistic problems (all students have a "front seat" for learning), and distance or obtaining experts is no barrier to "admission."	6. Relatively high cost of equipment and materials.
8. Can extend the boundaries of understanding through special techniques: slow motion, time lapse, telephotograph, animation, microphotography, multiple images, special effects, marriage of sight and sound, X-ray photograph, close-ups, filmographic techniques, and stop-motion.	7. Requires effective external light control.
9. 8mm cartridge has simplicity of operation and adaptability to single-concept, short-duration presentations.	8. Creates inconvenience in physical setup, operation and removal of equipment to "prevent" many teachers from availing themselves of one of the most potentially powerful educational tools.
10. 8mm can be used by small groups or individual students.	
11. Properly used, sound motion pictures can create a learning environment—emotionally and cognitively equalled by no other media.	

EDUCATIONAL AND INSTRUCTIONAL TELEVISION

1. Provides immediacy; brings the "here and now" of notable events to the audience as they occur.	1. Often involves passive watching and listening rather than active learning or application.
2. Reaches large groups or huge seg-	2. Often lacks programs of superior

Strengths

ments of the population with simultaneous presentations.

3. Provides outstanding instructors to larger audiences.

4. Provides information, presents ideas, and affects attitudes without requiring physical presence.

5. Provides programs that can be stored for retrieval, via video tapes, which retain a "live broadcast" feeling.

6. Combines visual and auditory involvement right in the home, classroom or study carrel.

7. Allows opportunities for group or individual study.

Weaknesses

educational quality; does not compare favorably with commercial television.

3. Often repeats mediocre or inferior teaching presentations on kinescope or video tape; can have a negative effect on the learning process.

4. Is often used as a substitute for employing good teachers and superior teaching procedures.

5. Requires adequate technical maintenance; many systems do not function well for lack of repair.

6. Often lacks the superior personnel required for local sophisticated TV facilities.

7. Generally limited to black and white and small picture size (21" or smaller); other media use color and large pictures.

A preliminary rating was designed by William H. Allen for the effectiveness of different instructional media types when used to accomplish six different learning objectives in art education.

Instructional Media Stimulus Relationships to Learning Objectives [1]

LEARNING OBJECTIVES:

INSTRUCTIONAL MEDIA TYPE:	Learning Factual Information	Learning Visual Identifications	Learning Principles, Concepts and Rules	Learning Procedures	Performing Skilled Perceptual-Motor Acts	Developing Desirable Attitudes, & Opinions
Still Pictures	Medium	HIGH	Medium	Medium	low	low
Motion Pictures	Medium	HIGH	HIGH	HIGH	Medium	Medium
Television	Medium	Medium	HIGH	Medium	low	Medium
3-D Objects	low	HIGH	low	low	low	low
Audio Recordings	Medium	low	low	Medium	low	Medium
Programed Instruction	Medium	Medium	Medium	HIGH	low	Medium
Demonstration	low	Medium	low	HIGH	Medium	Medium
Printed Textbooks	Medium	low	Medium	Medium	low	Medium
Oral Presentation	Medium	low	Medium	Medium	low	Medium

[1] William H. Allen, "Media Stimulus and Types of Learning," *Audiovisual Instruction* (January, 1967), p. 28.

This chart is useful as a starting point to analyze the nature of the instructional objectives and the teaching methods employed with the various media.

Practical Programs for Multimedia Teaching

With the advent of learning systems, multimedia, cross-media and packaged learning materials, several tongue-in-cheek media specialists and librarians have advocated an entirely new approach called *B*asic *O*rderly *O*rganized *K*nowledge, or BOOK, as it is more commonly known.

Fortunately, the battle of books versus media seems to have been won by both "sides" and the students are the real victors. Multiple texts, reference books and materials, "supermarket" shelves of paperbacks, and microfiche are among the printed, book-like materials that have been added to the newer "multimedia" or "cross-media" teaching-learning situations created by innovative teachers, media specialists, and librarians.

In considering the foregoing chart on media stimulus relationships to learning objectives, it would seem that selective and creative use of multiple materials and media for individuals and groups would move the ratings up for all types of learning objectives. One recent research project on the multimedia approach yielded conclusions that support the assumption that carefully programed multimedia units improve learning.

In the science vocabulary section of the study, the experimental groups showed greater gains—fifty-six per cent to 281 per cent more—than the control groups. In the social studies vocabulary section, the experimental groups again showed greater gains than the control groups—ranging from forty-six to 102 per cent.

It was concluded that the experimental groups that used the multimedia approach—16mm motion picture film, filmstrips, an opaque projector—showed larger vocabulary gains than the control groups not utilizing these multiple materials. The gains ranged from forty-six to 281 per cent.

Teachers reported that students exposed to the multimedia approach enjoyed the added interest of the lessons and, when tested six months later, were found to retain the vocabulary learned for longer periods than the students in the control groups.

It was interesting to note that according to diaries maintained by the students during the project, those students in the experimental group voluntarily engaged in more reading and other activities related to classwork than did those in the control group.

The findings of this research clearly indicate the advantages of the multimedia approach to increased learning.[2]

---

[2] Nicholas P. Georgiady, Louis G. Romano, and Walter A. Wittich, "Increased Learning Through the Multimedia Approach," *Audiovisual Instruction* (March, 1967).

This recent research will undoubtedly add to the continuing and often dramatic evidence that the use of single media techniques such as overhead projectors, film, filmstrips, radio, television, and audio tapes can increase teaching effectiveness and student achievements.[3]

Cross-media may be defined as the planned and systematic use of carefully selected multiple media devices and materials to enhance learning experiences. Each device and its coordinated materials is presented in that portion of a lesson or unit where it will be most effective in the teaching-learning process. The only limitation on the use of cross-media is the teacher's and the media specialist's imagination and ingenuity.

For years, ever since the value of media was first realized, a teacher was thought to be doing well if she utilized a projector, a phonograph or any

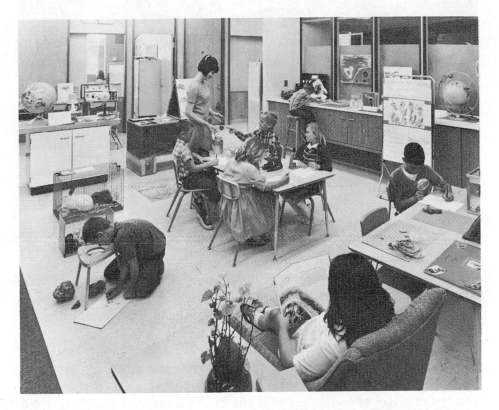

Photo 22. Individualized learning combined with small-group instruction in cross-media experiences. (Photograph courtesy of Fountain Valley School District, Fountain Valley, California.)

[3] James W. Brown, Richard B. Lewis, and Fred F. Harcleroad, *AV Instruction: Media and Methods* (New York: McGraw-Hill Book Company, 1969), pp. 198, 220, 256, 285, and 303.

Photo 23. Individualized learning combined with small-group instruction in cross-media experiences. (Bell & Howell, Audio Visual Products Division, Chicago, Illinois.)

one of the various "media" in her classes. All such items were considered useful teaching tools, and they still are. But if a teacher today were to use both a motion film and an overhead projector in the same class, then she would be approaching cross-media. If she were also to employ a bulletin board display, artifacts and perhaps a recording to teach various aspects of a single lesson to her class most effectively—then it can be said that the cross-media method of presentation has been used.

Example: A fifth-grade teacher is presenting a geography lesson on Switzerland. In her effort to make the country "come alive" for her class, she may use a Swiss film, several books and photographs, perhaps even twenty-five pieces of Swiss cheese! If she knows someone who has traveled throughout the country, she may arrange to borrow photos taken by that person.

Example: A high school class studying contemporary Egypt might have the benefit of a special kit of films depicting life along the Nile River, a swatch of Egyptian cotton fiber (which could be compared with domestic cotton), some recordings of Egyptian music, perhaps some costumes native to the country, reports of archaeologists who have made recent discoveries there, and projectuals of news clippings of civil strife, the Communist situation and the strained relations with Israel.

Examples: Rear-screen projection, slide films, motion films, recordings and other media are used to present lessons to large groups of students. The use of media can be controlled automatically or by a teacher who might be lecturing to the class simultaneously. In some related systems, students are able to respond to questioning by means of automatic scoring equipment located at each seat in the auditorium.

Students are effectively exposed to many more facts and concepts about their subject than was ever before possible either by a teacher who had no tools at all or by one limited to a projector, a phonograph or a display.

Of course, getting the material for cross-media use was more difficult. There had been no comprehensive listing of cross-referenced materials that could be correlated for a cross-media presentation until the Office of Educational Media Council compiled lists of all such materials. More than 100,000 items from more than 800 sources have been identified and sub-indexed by subject areas and/or educational levels. The listing includes kits, films, kinescopes, models, mock-ups, phono tapes, charts and graphs, programed instructional material, slides, and video tapes. In addition, an up-to-date index on 16mm films and 35mm slides has been added to these lists. Having a reference list like this available will certainly make it easier for a district to adopt the cross-media approach to teaching.

Using a Media System to Individualize Learning

Matching multiple materials and media to an individual student's ability, rate of learning, interest, and achievement levels is difficult under the best of circumstances. When a teacher is also asked to check availability, delivery systems, equipment, and operation, individualizing instruction is usually reduced to an occasional tailored homework assignment.

The Beverly Hills, California, school district has embarked on a retrieval system that provides teachers and students access to vast quantities of knowledge at the spin of a dial: without walking down the corridor to the library or the instructional materials center; without waiting in line for materials and equipment; and without setting up and taking down various pieces of relatively complicated hardware.

The Beverly Hills system now serves both the high school and all of the district's four elementary schools.

The basic components are:

1. A central studio that transmits sound and pictures via underground coaxial cables, having facilities for producing media materials. Equipment includes TV cameras, 16mm movie projectors, a 35mm slide and filmstrip projector, audio and video tape recorders, a turntable with amplifier, a microphone, a switching and distribution system and an intercom hookup with the viewing stations in the schools, and TV transmission and control facilities.

2. Classroom viewing stations—five in the high school and four in the elementary schools—that are connected to the information retrieval system. Each station has a twenty-five-inch TV receiver, a speaker, an amplifier, and a wall panel containing a dial selector, intercom facilities with the central studio, volume control, a button to advance slides, and a button to "clear" the circuit prior to dialing for material.

3. Eight study carrel viewing stations—in the high school library. Each carrel has a nine-inch TV receiver, a headset and a control panel identical to those used in the classrooms.

How would a teacher and student use such a system to individualize instruction? At the point where a teacher and student have agreed upon an assignment, "contract," or other task based upon the student's ability, interest, rate of growth, and current achievement levels, the student can consult the district catalog, a widely distributed mimeographed list of all the media materials in stock. The student may then select a film on life in Tokyo today to obtain the proper orientation for his assignment on the study of economics in modern Japan. The student then visits the studio and requests the film for showing later that afternoon.

The technician notes the request and assigns the student a two-digit number that will activate one of the studio's two 16mm projectors.

A member of the studio staff then obtains the film from storage and threads the film on the projector. From there on everything is fully automatic.

In the study carrel the student simply presses the "reset" button to clear the circuit and then dials the two-digit number. Within a matter of seconds, the film on Tokyo flashes on the screen. In the studio the pre-assigned two-digit number activates the TV signal from the studio to the carrel and also starts the movie projector. The film is projected directly into a TV camera mounted in front of the projector. The projector shuts off automatically at the end of the reel.

Unlike conventional closed-circuit TV systems that can accommodate only one program at a time, this system can carry thirteen programs simultaneously—eight video and five audio. This number can be expanded as needed.

Each viewing station, regardless of where it is, receives programs independently of other viewing stations. This gives the teacher or student complete freedom to see, or hear, the material he wants when he wants it.

Finally, the system can tune in on all commercial TV channels and on the local UHF educational channel.

The system is operated by five full-time employees: a director of instructional materials who has responsibility for the overall project; two materials specialists (one for elementary school and one for high school) who are responsible for the production of materials; a technician who directs control room operations; and a graphics artist who specializes in the preparation of filmstrips and slides. In addition, the studio uses as many as ten part-time student helpers for such tasks as threading projectors, obtaining material from storage and taping programs for future use.

How does the use of this media system individualize learning? The techniques and approaches are limited only by the teacher's and student's imagination. In fact, creativity is fostered through use and desire to delve deeper into a topic or subject of interest. Some examples of both service functions and unusual uses of this type of retrieval system include:

1. make-up of work missed through absence;
2. learning assigned and advanced science-lab techniques;
3. drilling in pronunciation and grammar;
4. independent study "contracts";
5. self-scheduled assignments;
6. viewing live and taped news broadcasts;
7. building knowledge in special areas of interest, e.g., architecture, law, economics;
8. broadcasting original student performances, programs, "teaching" lessons, and documentaries;
9. student-to-student tutoring tapes; and
10. simulation games in social studies and other disciplines.

In every instance an individual student and teacher can plan a learning program or contract for individual pacing and achievement. Further, individual students can progress with or without reference to other students, groups and teachers—depending on the type of instructional contract design established.

Santa Barbara and Palo Alto, California, Stayton, Oregon, and West

Hartford, Connecticut are other districts that have moved strongly into various retrieval systems. Lake Forest, Illinois, high school utilizes a dial code select system through the Illinois Bell Telephone system. Thirty-two different programs may be dialed every night between 5 and 11 P.M. from anywhere in the country—the switching system was invented by a junior student at the high school!

If your district cannot afford these types of sophisticated media systems it should begin to analyze the functions served and to design less costly media programs to meet these needs. For example, inexpensive tapes, cassettes and player-recorders can be checked out to students or used in assigned areas of the library or resource center. Students can tutor each other by this method without requiring a complex retrieval system.

The authors strongly recommend Bloom's *Taxonomy of Educational Objectives: Cognitive Domain* [4] and Mager's *Preparing Instructional Objectives* [5] as key guides for teachers who wish to know how to individualize instruction. The use of media in workshops should follow understanding and practice with the categories, terms and procedures described in the two books. For example, Mager states that:

1. A statement of instructional objectives is a collection of words or symbols describing one of your educational intents.
2. An objective will communicate your intent to the degree you have described what the learner will be Doing when demonstrating his achievement and how you will know when he is doing it.
3. To describe terminal behavior (what the learner will be Doing):
   a. Identify and name the over-all behavior act.
   b. Define the important conditions under which the behavior is to occur (givens and/or restrictions and limitations).
   c. Define the criterion of acceptable performance. [6]

Media can offer major assistance in defining and following through on each procedure, teaching technique, learning response and evaluation of acceptable performance.

---

[4] Benjamin S. Bloom (ed.), *Taxonomy of Educational Objectives* (New York: David McKay Co., 1956).

[5] Robert E. Mager, *Preparing Instructional Objectives* (Palo Alto, Calif.: Fearon Publishers, 1962).

[6] *Ibid.,* p. 53.

Four Ideas for Student Resource Centers

Classroom resources, facilities and management for the teacher were discussed in chapter 2. Resources for each student will receive increasing attention as the trend toward individualization accelerates. Organizational plans for middle schools, nongrading, modular and flexible scheduling, independent study, team teaching, team learning, and "dispersed" schooling all involve the development of resources and the use of levels of achievement measurement for individual students in ever increasing quantity and quality.

The four specific design ideas for student resources that follow were developed for different purposes and with total expenditures that are within the reach of the majority of school systems in the country.

1. *Utilizing present or planned classrooms.*—The Garden City, New York, high school center consists of three "planned" classrooms and a small portion of the library that is adjacent. A few partitions were removed, and the entire area was divided into space for twenty-four individual carrels, a vision panel utilizing a rear-screen projection system, and a production and equipment center for developing, producing and storing media materials.

The carrels are built in six clusters. Each cluster contains four carrels, radiating from a common central leg. Each is electrically wired for listening. If a student wants to listen to records or tapes, he obtains a headset from the nearby issue counter. A "librarian" "connects" the listener to the record or tape at the issue center.

Each carrel can receive a different recording, or the same material can be piped out to many carrels simultaneously.

The "vision panel" is a pane of ground glass fourteen feet wide and one foot high set into a floor-to-ceiling partition. Students sit on one side of the partition to view films; projection equipment is set up on the other side about eight feet away from one of the center's permanent walls. Two more partitions run at right angles from the vision panel to box off the chamber from the rest of the center. A built-in door is the only means of access.

The "vision room" is lined with shelves that house a series of rear-screen projectors. When a student wishes to view a film he submits his request to an aide at the issue counter. He is furnished with a headset and given a seat facing the glass panel. The aide then sets up the projector behind the panel. The opaque glass strip becomes the viewing screen, the headset transmits sound and blocks out extraneous noise. When the film ends the student returns the headset to the issue counter. The aide then returns to shut off the projector, but no one has to be in the vision room while the film is being viewed.

The vision panel provides many of the advantages of a movie theater, yet retains the privacy of television. As many as six or seven students can view different films simultaneously, with no cross-over of sight or sound. Several students can view the same film together by connecting their headsets into the same sound track.

The center is staffed as simply as it is designed. One librarian operates the resource center's issue counter. The school's media coordinator is in charge of producing materials and supervising equipment in the center. Approximately twenty-five to thirty students work part time distributing equipment and materials in the center.

The design and function of this resource center are inexpensive, practical and useful.

2. *Making Media Come Alive.*—A media aid can be almost anything that helps a teacher teach and a learner learn. It can be something as sophisticated as multiple-image television—or as primitive as a snake.

Live African snakes, rats and other animals as well as insects and plants are proof that media is alive and well in a ninth-grade student resource center in a Jericho, New York, junior high school. Media, in this case, are living proof of what can be done for a group of highly motivated students interested in African culture. The teacher stated that students rarely understand a culture that is vastly different from their own personal experiences. The solution to this problem was suggested by the students themselves: to make the African portion of this Afro-Asian culture series more meaningful, why not bring a slice of Africa right into the room?

Students volunteered to write letters and ask for needed materials. In fact, they paid "dues," with the teacher also contributing to cover the expenses of this instructional approach. (The school now budgets funds for this resource center.) "We emphasized getting live samples of various plant and animal life directly from Africa. Much of the culture of Africa can be effectively taught, using these elements as starting points," stated the teacher, Emil Voight.

To establish the resource center Voight and his students divided the classroom into two equal spaces. One area became a "miniature Africa," containing everything live or inanimate the class could obtain that reflected African culture.

The students, after contacting every African government and every airline that flew to Africa, secured over 300 living specimens—everything from a species of small crocodile to a climbing vine that now flows over most of the resource center.

Meanwhile, parents and the community-at-large joined the local safari by donating fish tanks, cages, African masks, and other appropriate realia.

The first week of class in this "blackboard jungle" was almost chaotic. New students were over-stimulated about the new resource center. They and the teacher had to become accustomed to living with the specimens, and the specimens had to adapt to the students!

Photo 24. Making media come alive. (Photograph used with permission of the publisher of *School Management* Magazine, copyright 1968, 1969, Management Publishing Group, Inc.)

There were also some qualms among parents about their thirteen-year-old children fraternizing with a fourteen-foot python. According to the teacher, "The fear and hatred of snakes illustrates a culture gap. Everything in our cultural system makes us dislike the snake intensely. Yet, in Africa he is a beneficial creature. He is raised on farms there and sold as a pet. And he earns his keep by keeping homes free of rats and vermin."

Voight spent a week letting his students become acclimated. They learned safety rules for handling specimens and were assigned independent research projects.

A typical research project developed was "Religions of Kenya." Students learned that over eighty per cent of the religious ceremonies in that country

Photo 25. Making media come alive. (Photograph used with permission of the publisher of *School Management* Magazine, copyright 1968, 1969, Management Publishing Group, Inc.)

involve animals and, therefore, a true relationship between its culture and its animal life exists.

The non-jungle half of this resource center includes more conventional media materials, e.g., filmstrips and slides related to the live specimens, many of which were produced by the instructor and the students attending the center.

This type of living resource center teaches self-reliance and responsibility. Highly motivated students maintain the animals and plants, keeping proper humidity and oxygen levels that parallel those of the native environment. When cages and floors have to be cleaned, the students do it all and, rather than complain, they work extra hours—even during weekends.

Most parents overcome their qualms as they observe newly emerged self-confidence and involvement in their children. When twelve- and thirteen-year-old girls handle fourteen-foot snakes like dolls, it is evident that fear based on lack of knowledge has been erased by living experiences. ("Besides, a python has to be twenty feet long, at least, to be even remotely dangerous," claimed the teacher.)

3. *Orbiting Satellite Resource Center.*—The New Medford, Massachu-

setts, high school enrolls 3,000 students in a comprehensive program. The building, like the curriculum, is departmentalized. Separate wings house separate departments, with their own satellite resource centers. The concept places specific learning materials in the spaces rather than in one large instructional media center (IMC).

The satellite resource center in the science area of the school, for example, is a long, rectangular room in the middle of a cluster of science (biology, physics, chemistry) classrooms. The resource center includes lab tables, carrels (connected to the main IMC's audio resources), storage space for experimentation equipment, books, tapes, and other materials; an area for preparing instructional materials; a darkroom; and a vivarium.

There is direct access to the center from classrooms and hallway. It is located near the department lecture hall and the IMC, which is directly underneath on the first floor.

This resource center is a "satellite" to both the science department facilities and the IMC. It is a satellite to the department because it is located and equipped for independent study in science, and science alone. It is a satellite to the main IMC because it obviates the need to provide, centrally, in-depth services in the sciences. The IMC can, therefore, be commensurately smaller and designed to better service all departments.

Teachers in the science department are able to use their resource center in at least four ways: as a lesson preparation area; as an independent study area for students who are working at their own pace; as a remedial area; and as a small-group discussion and work area, supplementing the lecture hall and classroom spaces in the science wing.

With similar laboratory-carrel areas stocked with pertinent materials and equipment for each departmental area of the school, students and teachers have what they need to make optimum use of free time and "study periods."

Medford schoolmen are counting on the thesis that when it is possible for students to do something constructive with their free time, they will.

Again, if cost is a factor begin by examining existing budgets and classrooms near the library or near departmental clusters of rooms. Some inexpensive redesigning may produce satellite resource centers. (See chapter 2 for design suggestions.)

4. *Using Student Power.*—The problem: a germinating independent study program . . . but no physical base of operation for it in the school.

The solution: change a cafeteria into an independent research center—and let students do a major share of the planning and building. This was a deliberate attempt to involve the student body—potential dropouts and honor students—in the new thrust toward independent study. And it worked at the H. W. Smith Junior High School at Syracuse, New York.

In order to find the required space for the center, the school principal used one of the school's two cafeterias. He did this by simply scheduling more lunch sessions in the remaining cafeteria.

Instructional equipment for the center was selected during meetings of administrators and faculty. But when it came to the furnishings, students took the lead.

The principal scheduled a number of meetings with youngsters who comprised a cross-section of interests and asked for their ideas on designing the center.

The students had one common complaint: they could not get comfortable while studying in school. Some of them liked to read books on the floor. Others favored a lounge or swivel chair. A few said they hated hard seats.

Among other suggestions: students should be able to walk around, stretch their legs, or take a conversation break between classes. They needed a quiet atmosphere, plus some means of visual privacy. On the other hand, they did not wish to feel hemmed in.

These suggestions were taken seriously in designing the resource center. The center has several low tables, which allow students to be on the floor while reading—seated on pillows. A "conversation corner" is set aside in one remote corner, with a plush sectional. Swivel and semi-upholstered chairs are carefully distributed. And twenty-five carrels provide visual isolation.

To counteract that "hemmed-in" feeling, every furnishing and piece of equipment is removable—hardly a carrel or a counter is nailed down. The center's furnishings thus can be rearranged to meet changing student needs.

Quiet is assured by three soundproofing techniques: two walls are covered with cork (which establishes a gigantic "bulletin board"); windows are covered with heavy drapes; and the floor is carpeted.

The major construction work was done by outside professionals. In the making of interior furnishings, however, the principal selected students who seemed almost certain to be school dropouts. They were offered the project of planning and making the tables, carrels and desks for the center, under the tutelage of an industrial arts instructor.

These youngsters volunteered to go to school after regular classes to learn about designing and building furniture.

During the summer, before the center opened, they were hired to draw up final plans and build the furnishings. For much of this work, they were paid $1.25 per hour under the terms of a federal project.

Field trips to lumber yards and cabinetmakers were incorporated into this summer training to give the students orientation to the work and the costs. The carrels they ultimately designed for the center were based on an idea they saw at the nearby college.

Part of the success of the resource center project can be measured by the eight out of ten potential dropout students who stayed in school.

"Without the resource center work project there was a chance we would have lost them all," stated the principal.

Saving "FACE": Film Activities for Creative Education

Films have long been underrated for their ability to involve students in experiences that seem real and important to them. One proposal to capitalize on this potential was prepared by co-author Kenneth Dunn, John M. Culkin, S.J., and William Zeralsky. The main elements of the plan centered on the hypothesis that improvement of the audience would lead to increased effectiveness of the medium.

The rationale for the proposal was based on the concept that we live in a media-saturated society. The term media includes television, painting, music, sculpture, advertising of all kinds, radio, computers, cartoons, plays, films, photography, opera, ballet, telephones, architecture, tape recorders, phonographs, speech, printing, and other related forms of communication. Students spend thousands of hours watching television, listening to the radio, reading newspapers and magazines, and being involved with other media. They live in a total environment rather than in a series of independent fragments. This environment belongs to this century. Within our century we have moved from a speech- and print-dominated culture into a total information and polymedia culture. Intelligent living within such a culture demands an understanding of all of these media.

For the first time in history, information levels are higher outside the classroom than in it. The student lives in both these worlds. What is unified in his experience should also be unified in his understanding. A general challenge arises that can be stated in two ways:

1. To improve the student through media.
2. To improve media through the student.

The first stresses the positive contribution of the rich and varied experiences available to the student through all the media. The second underscores the fact that the media, especially the commercially exploited ones, respond to the demands of their audience; therefore, improve the audience and you improve the medium.[7]

---

[7] Adapted from an unpublished position paper entitled, "A Proposal on Understanding Media," used with the permission of the author, John M. Culkin, S.J., Director of the Center for Communications, Fordham University; paper delivered to Board of Education, City of New York, May 14, 1967.

Project FACE (Film Activities for Creative Education) would provide opportunities for teachers and students to study one of the media—films— and through it, to develop understanding of all media.

Project FACE would take a communication medium enjoyed by youngsters and use it as a vehicle, to get through to them, to motivate them, to help them learn things about their world.[8]

"We know today's kids are shaped a great deal by the film media, they know more about their world while in elementary school than their great-grandparents ever got to know." [9]

We have all seen children glued to a movie or a TV screen sharing with the film or TV personalities their frustrations, joys and sorrows, victories and defeats. We have seen them become kings, poets, spacemen, saints, clowns, cowboys, Indians, and good guys and bad guys. We have seen them transported to different lands, homes and cultures. We have seen many of their personal decisions shaped by films. Through this medium we have seen fads, symbols, and styles of dress develop. And we have seen values shaped by the film and TV medium. We have also seen them exposed to a great deal of nonsense and mediocrity.

What might happen if schools were to utilize the untapped knowledge that students bring into the schools—through the film medium? What discussions might take place? What new roads might be opened? What doors might be unlocked for a society changing so rapidly? What might happen if schools were to show movie and TV films, effectively and meaningfully discuss them, teach them, make them?

Marshall McLuhan (holder of the Albert Schweitzer Chair at Fordham University) in his book *Understanding Media* expresses the feeling that very few people really see the present because of limited perception. We tend to miss seeing the present because we translate it into the past; yet so many of our most pressing problems deal with the *present*.

1. Our modes of cognition and perception are influenced by the culture we are in now. Even our language is determined by the media to which we are exposed. Can we begin to solve some of our present problems by having students see and understand the present through the medium of the movie and TV screen?
2. Would students who become discouraged and alienated by the unreal environment of school take on new interests?

---

[8] John M. Culkin, S.J., "A Schoolman's Guide to Marshall McLuhan," *Saturday Review* (March 18, 1967).

[9] John M. Culkin, S.J., "I Was a Teen-Age Movie Teacher," *Saturday Review* (July 16, 1966).

3. Would students with diverse backgrounds (advantaged and disadvantaged) gain new insights into their problems and assets and be helped toward their understanding and growth?
4. Can the interest generated through film activities spill over to other media?
5. Would more analytical, discerning audiences be created? Walt Whitman said, "To have great poets there must be a great audience." Surely, if we improve the audience the arts will also improve.

The objectives of the program were:

1. To utilize the realistic and motivating influences of films in building better audiences.
2. To sharpen student perceptions and to teach analysis skills.
3. To create an awareness of quality and beauty.
4. To provide students with new insights into familiar experiences.
5. To close the gap between the classroom and the outside world.
6. To close the gap between generations by involving adults with students.
7. To produce enthusiastic, selective and mature film viewers.
8. To use the film to build perception, appreciation and understanding of the other arts, e.g., music, painting, ballet.
9. To develop more intelligent use of other media such as television, radio, telephone, or recordings.
10. To provide orientation and guidance for the vocational opportunities in the film and allied industries.
11. To produce films using student writers, directors, producers, actors, and technologists.
12. To provide knowledge of film history, techniques, production, and economics.
13. To utilize the film in reaching and motivating the disadvantaged and other students who are not learning through our traditional approach to their problems or academic deficiencies.
14. To involve the students and community in film festivals and to add to their growth and understanding of society and their future.
15. To provide in-service courses for teachers on the analysis and teaching of films.

The procedures to achieve these objectives would be as follows:

1. Fifty teachers from different schools, subject areas and grade levels would be selected to participate in continuing training in the art and teaching of the film. As part of the first planning phase,

teacher teams would be selected from disciplines such as guidance, English, social studies, science, industrial arts, and audiovisual arts, since media cut across all academic disciplines.

The teachers would:

a. see examples of excellence.

b. receive training in non-directive discussion techniques.

c. learn of the film relationship to other arts.

d. be introduced to the techniques that are intrinsic to the medium—editing, lighting, composition, framing, dialogue, sound effects, music, color, and screen size.

e. be acquainted with the roles of the individuals involved in the making of a film—producer, director, art director, film editor, cinematographer, screen writer, and sound artist.

f. learn of the history of film and its technical and artistic development.

g. learn to use norms for evaluating films and television and to relate these new media to the norms for criticism in literature and the arts.

h. be given practical suggestions on how screen education can be introduced into the school and how it can be integrated with subjects in the curriculum.

i. be trained to organize in-service programs for other teachers and to explore experimental screen education programs and film teaching materials.

j. be introduced to opportunities for student film making.

2. Teachers, professionals in the film industry and community leaders would sponsor and attend festivals of selected and appropriate films.

3. Students of the teachers in training would participate in similar festivals and attendance would overlap on certain films.

4. Teaching materials such as film clips, prints, video tapes, television assignments, study guides, demonstrations, and evaluation kits would be developed for teachers and students and, in later phases of the project, by teachers and students.

5. Films and professionals "in-residence" would be established for participants and interested observers.

6. Outstanding directors, actors, producers, and other professionals would work with the institute, teachers and students in fulfilling the objectives.

7. Students and teachers would visit TV and movie studios.

8. Students and teachers would prepare to make films during the operational phase, e.g.,

Documentary:	"Where and How We Live," "Who Am I?" "What Is Our World?"
Imaginative:	"What I Would Like to Be or Do," "What School Ought to Be," "My Son in 1984."
Abstract:	"Painting on Film," "Motion Through Stills," "Meaning Through Sound Without Words."
Commentary:	"Happenings in Our Society."

9. Institute officials, teachers, students and community leaders would evaluate the project and plan for extension into wider training, production and operational phases.

10. School guidance personnel would work with film institute participants on the educational, personal and vocational needs of student participants.

This project was approved for federal funding but was never consummated by the submitting school district. In the opinion of the authors, the proposal involves the wise use of technology to serve students. Someone should try it!

The New Technology: Look Before You Leap

The electronic classroom of the future seems to promise instantaneous retrieval of recordings, films, video tapes, filmstrips, slides, and books. Drawings by computer and "through pictures" projected to a large wall screen by the flick of a switch, a dial or even by voice command will be commonly accepted procedures.

Transition to this wondrous day is still remote, however—perhaps ten to twenty years for most schools. At this date, enormous sums would be required to implement that which our technology has made possible. Further, educators are not ready to use the new equipment. Moreover, needs vary for different students and areas, and programs must be tailored to local needs and consumers must be involved early.

Other specific problems include:

1. *Storage.*—Storage of vastly different media is unwieldly and retrieval is limited. Records, books, slides, tapes, and films must be stacked carefully in different places and in ways that are compatible to maintenance, replacement and systems efficiency.

2. *Retrieval.*—Coaxial cables can carry only twelve or twenty-one separate programs simultaneously which, thus far, limits the number of

programs and transmissions available. Common carriers have not yet been developed.

3. *Equipment.*—Most television screens are still small and project black and white pictures; color, although advancing steadily, is still unperfected and not in widespread use in education.

4. *Personnel.*—Skilled and efficient media specialists, trainers of teachers, and administrators are necessary to assist you in the leap—or plunge. The "new technology" *is* new, and costly. Try to prepare for the launching as far ahead as possible and invest wisely to serve all of the students effectively.

Television Cartridge Systems: A Promising Development

One promising new development for the 70's and 80's is the television cartridge system (TCS). Devices which record and play back televised material through the use of cartridges could aid small-group, independent study and individualized instruction to take another large leap forward.

The new system will permit prerecorded material to be played through conventional television sets from small, easy-to-use cartridges or discs inserted into portable electronic devices attached to the antenna ends of television sets. The cost of the new devices will vary from $120 to $1000, and the cartridges will sell for about $20 to $30 each. Another innovation being developed is a video disc which will allow playback only, but the advantage would be its low cost. The player will cost between $120 and $350, and the discs will sell for approximately one dollar or less.

The low cost of the system and materials should permit the widespread development and adoption of good video-instructional materials such as the programs produced for the successful "Sesame Street" series. In this regard schools are being pressed more and more by industry to improve the quality and relevance of current instructional programs. Television cartridge systems offer another medium that challenges the educational establishment to better its performance and offerings.

8

Making the New Media
Work for School
and Community

Supervising Media for the Disadvantaged

Reaching the Unreachables

They are everywhere—in every district, in every school, in virtually every classroom. They are not necessarily either hard-core discipline cases or "slow learners." They are disadvantaged students who simply are not interested in school. It is difficult to motivate them to participate in educational activities and, partially because of their lack of involvement, they do not achieve well academically. They seem to be—unreachable.

Bushnell observed that art experiences such as film making for dropouts and potential dropouts in Watts, North Philadelphia and New York resulted in improved student interaction with others, improved self-image, personal identification with a positive role model, increased self-perception, assimilation of skills and related knowledge, better perception of peers and community, and motivation to pursue constructive activities such as voluntarily returning to school, obtaining employment, and passing a driving test.[1]

---

[1] Don D. Bushnell, "The Educational Advantages of the Poor," *Audiovisual Instruction* (January, 1968), p. 27.

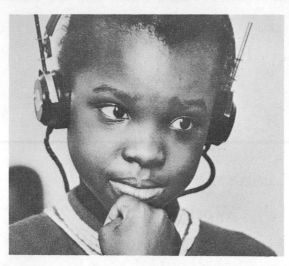

Photo 26.   Reaching every student. (Bell & Howell, Audio Visual Products Division, Chicago, Illinois.)

Other art-oriented activities for the disadvantaged that are taking root in many sections of the country are sponsored by drama groups, dance workshops, storefront theaters, television production enterprises, neighbor-

Photo 27.   TV commercials: the task should be student-centered. (Photograph used with permission of the publisher of *School Management* Magazine, copyright 1968, 1969, Management Publishing Group, Inc.)

hood artists and musical theater clubs. Media plays a strong role in each of these communications experiences through the emphasis on arts activities. Indeed, it is difficult to separate art from communication, and communication is essential to motivation and the process of education.

In addition to art experiences (or their usage as an introduction to learning), "unreachable" youngsters should be provided opportunities to produce their own media materials using school media equipment. The students should use media tools and be made responsible for them as well as the project on which the equipment is being used.

Many items are available at low cost:

1. Small, durable, low-cost tape recorders are now available in both lightweight and easy-to-operate models. Some use cartridge tapes. These units can be taken "on location" by students to record audio tapes, interviews, short plays, readings, and dramatic events.

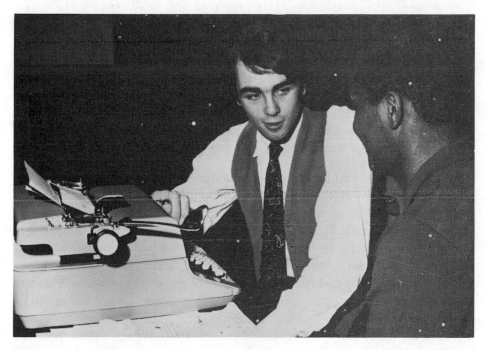

Photo 28. Approval and interest should be sought and obtained from peers. (Photograph used with permission of the publisher of *School Management* Magazine, copyright 1968, 1969, Management Publishing Group, Inc.)

2. The Polaroid camera is another inexpensive, easy-to-operate tool with one particularly appealing feature—instant results. Students can take and "develop" black-and-white pictures in minutes. For youngsters who need to improve their self-image with peers or who

seek to create a positive image of their school, their environment or their community, the Polaroid camera can be an extremely effective device.

3. The 35mm cameras, for the most part, are not expensive. The newer models are now easy to operate and often include automatic meter settings. Although many 35mm cameras are still relatively delicate instruments, some of the lower priced models are built to withstand extremely heavy duty. Youngsters can learn to use these for creating slide-sound presentations, color prints, filmstrips, exhibits, and displays.

4. Film kits, which include complete "scratch and doodle" equipment consisting of black and clear 16mm film, scratch pins, colored markers, splicer and tape as well as an instructional manual, are now available for exciting and creative "moving art." Music, communications, mathematics, and science may also be launched by this approach. Disadvantaged youngsters are captivated by their own instantaneous creations to which background music may be added via cassette recorders.

5. Motion picture cameras, particularly 8mm cameras, are available at moderate cost for taking action pictures. No particular expertise is needed other than that usually acquired from basic instruction and some experience. Students can project themselves into their communities and involve local residents so that a positive interrelationship is established and experienced.

While the use of simple media equipment as described above would benefit all students, these techniques offer disadvantaged youngsters unprecedented opportunities to record information and "slices of life" essentially of their own choosing. In most schools they are rarely asked to concentrate on their own environment and are further handicapped because of lack of equipment. All curricular areas (particularly language arts and social studies) can easily be incorporated into any of the media projects that may develop from this relevant approach to learning in and from their environment.

There are many examples of school-coordinated assignments to motivate the disadvantaged:

1. *Field Trips.* Rather than have the entire class go on the same field trip, send groups of youngsters—accompanied, perhaps, by one or two certified substitute teachers and one or two aides or parents—on field trips tailored to their particular interests. These youngsters could record their experiences as communication teams using vary-

Photo 29. The teacher or aide should be an ally or helper who teaches skills and helps in producing or creating the presentation. (Photograph used with permission of the publisher of *School Management* Magazine, copyright 1968, 1969, Management Publishing Group, Inc.)

ing media equipment. Their work could then be presented to the rest of the class or other classes in the school.

2. *Community Assignments*. In the lower grades, social studies assignments on "community helpers" can take the form of taped interviews "on location." The fire chief, physicians, superintendent of schools, policemen, and city officials can answer questions on their functions and specific community problems. The Polaroid or a 35mm camera can be used to take pictures during the interview and, later, to photograph the areas discussed. This material can then be brought back for incorporation into a curriculum presentation with possible additional use in motivating future experience.

3. *Special Assignments*. A committee of youngsters can be given the assignment of covering local elections, observing the campaign, at-

tending meetings, photographing the voting machines, and interviewing and tape recording candidates and people waiting in line to vote. All of this reportorial action can be brought back to the class for general use and discussion.

The development of "TV commercials" and short films about the neighborhood and themselves are two of the limitless number of ways to use media in motivating the seemingly unreachable students. The benefits to disadvantaged students are many if the arts and media approach is used. The projects should incorporate many of the following concepts:

1. the task should be student-centered and not program- or teacher-directed.

Photo 30. Student self-image can be improved enormously by the triple threat of relevance, reality and results. (Photograph used with permission of the publisher of *School Management* Magazine, copyright 1968, 1969, Management Publishing Group, Inc.)

2. approval and interest should be sought and obtained from peers.
3. ideally, discipline should be self-imposed, not enforced.
4. the teacher or aide should be an ally or helper who teaches skills and helps in producing or creating the presentation.
5. student self-image can be improved enormously by the triple thrust of relevance, reality and results.

6. cognitive knowledge can be acquired painlessly and joyfully.
7. real "payoffs" in the form of money from sales, performances or job training may result.[2]

Keeping Students in School

There are many reasons for keeping students in school, but few solutions have been advanced that also describe how. The following are some practical media programs that have proven successful in keeping students in school.

Plainview, New York, introduced a modified work-study program within the school. Marginal students were employed in a media workshop that produced printed materials, transparencies, sound motion pictures, slides, and other materials. This modified work-study program involved students for three hours each day at a low but acceptable hourly rate of pay. Technicians in the media department worked with the students on jobs ranging through such areas as offset printing, industrial photography, and book production. The result of their work was a stream of useful materials that approached high commercial quality and were sometimes below commercial cost. Training occasionally led to employment in the media field.

Hempstead, New York, created a media study center after school. An attractive and lively learning place for slow learners was established. It was stocked with exciting equipment, colorful and dynamic materials and helpful tutors. It was open after school, at night and on Saturdays. Attendance was *voluntary*. Numerous study carrels were available for those who wished private sanctuary. Typing stations, tape recorders, record players, photocopiers, listening stations, film and filmstrip projectors, reference books, encyclopedias, atlases, magazines, dictionaries, almanacs, and newspapers were included. The center was carpeted and paneled, and the students were given the responsibility of keeping it immaculate. It was staffed with a director, or counselor, tutors, paraprofessionals, and groups of honor students at different times. Friendly persuasion and "marketing" techniques increased attendance when notices and word of mouth were slow in attracting "customers." A media center such as this can prevent some students from dropping out and aid others in improving their performance.

South Huntington, New York, scheduled media materials into students' homes. Students were permitted to requisition from the library 8mm single-concept films, filmstrips, records, audio tapes, and the appropriate equipment to view and hear them in the same manner as they would obtain books. Filmstrips on Greece, 8mm films on French pronunciation, audio tapes of

---

[2] Based on a list by Bushnell, *ibid.*, p. 25.

great modern poets, and 8mm films on typing are but a few of the thousands of films, strips and tapes that could be made available for home viewing and reviewing until learning occurs.

Various programs around the country would seem to indicate that students tend to treat articles entrusted to them like family "heirlooms." Tape recorders increase home-school communications, improve speech patterns, and stimulate creativity. Parents can hear what occurs in the classroom and send audio messages to the teacher. Students are strongly motivated to improve their speech and "sound like announcers." Creative writing, reading and narrations can result from any observed experience.

Most students are curious and naturally media oriented. Raise their expectations and aspirations by raising yours. Place media equipment and materials in their hands and watch students "turn on" and stay in school.

Six Administrative Gems

A Written System for Action, Not Reporting

Media supervisors, specialists, principals, and superintendents too often collect information and reports that are less than stimulating or useful to boards of education, the community and their own staffs. These reports usually include dry statistics on pieces of equipment used, inventories of new purchases, and an appeal for additional personnel, without convincing justification. Some simple criteria should be considered and established by a joint group of administrators, teachers, media specialists, board members, community residents, and students, all of whom are concerned with *writing and receiving a report that is meaningful and appropriate for making decisions to improve educational programs*. A list of items that might be used to begin a meeting of such a joint group is included here for consideration.

1. *Obtain Uniformity*. Establish a standardized sequence. Reports on overhead projectors, for example, would consistently appear in the same section of the report.
2. *Develop Logical Categories*. Design a report structure that reflects a rational breakdown of sections and items. Consider your current budget coding system, filing arrangements or curriculum and teaching reports for possible clues to organization.
3. *Insist on Accessibility*. Information for justifications, comparisons, analyses and other uses must be readily and easily retrievable. Use color-coded sheets, number tabs, cross indexing, chronological date files, and other techniques to insure rapid accessibility.
4. *Establish Priorities*. Develop a list of weighted priorities and use those

for length and placement of sections. Instructional items would be rated more important than equipment or supplies and be given more space earlier in the report. In the same manner, personnel needs would be given a higher priority than schedules.

5. *Schedule Planning Sessions.* Involve the staff, administrators, students, board members, and even the community if all of these groups constitute part of the audience for the reports. Use task teams to gather data, requests, suggestions, analyses, and other material for action-oriented reports.

6. *Review All Statements.* Assign readers to correct drafts and upgrade reports. Schedule workshops to improve reports by avoiding generalizations, by using specific observations and justifications, and by writing clear recommendations and evaluations.

7. *Establish Purposes.* Develop skills through workshops and evaluation of former reports in stating needs, goals, procedures, evaluations, and modifications. Learn to give reasons for requested improvements.

8. *Develop Interest.* Use effective media presentations to focus on important sections of the report or to highlight a single topic.

9. *Placement of Data.* Relegate lengthy support data and tables to the appendix. Refer to the "support evidence," but retain a more stimulating style for the main body of the report. Schedules, inventories, attendance figures, frequency-of-use charts, test data, etc., might all be placed in the appendix. Recommendations and summaries would be written in the appropriate sections at the front.

The report may be the very vehicle to aid policy and administrative groups in making decisions. One type of report might use a "problem-solving" approach, another, the "proposal" format:

1. *The Problem-Solving Approach*

   a. *Define the problem.* Analyze the problem in depth. Use specific examples, case studies, surveys, comments, interviews, evidence for, and examples that reveal the nature of the problem. Relate appropriate problem components to other areas of the total setting.

   b. *Design alternate solutions.* Vary appropriate components to determine possible strategies. Use teams to "brainstorm" action solutions without editorial comment. Explore many alternatives including the addition of new components, such as paraprofessionals, different organizational patterns and restructured budgets.

   c. *Recommend action.* Select one or two sets of general action procedures that would allow flexibility on the paths to solution of the problem.

   d. *Project the outcomes.* Support the recommendation with projected results. This will aid decision making and provide a tool for evaluation. It might prove beneficial to "simulate" future results.

   e. *Implement approved action procedures.* Use teams to develop detailed and viable procedures for implementing the proposed action solutions. Include every step, but build in checkpoints, schedules and flexible systems to insure paths that reach successful conclusions.

   f. *Report pertinent data.* Use reports and newsletters to keep all con-concerned informed and involved. Continue surveys and interviews as follow-up evaluation to modify procedures and implementation as necessary.

2. *The Proposal Format*

   a. *Establish the need.* Relate the need to the actual background of the community. Determine the cause of need—educational, social, instructional, economic, cultural, lack of opportunities, or other lack —peculiar to the situation.

   b. *Determine the objectives.* Design objectives that, if fully realized, will serve to fill the needs established. There should be a direct relationship to need. All objectives should be structured in terms that can be evaluated. (When goals are reached they should be observable and measurable.)

   c. *Develop the procedures.* Include every step that must be taken— facilities, staff, training, continuous reporting, pilot operations, preliminary preparations, calendars, measurement, evaluation, possible modification points, etc.

   d. *Design the evaluation.* Determine the extent to which objectives have been reached and state conclusions and recommendations that will assist the decision-making process for new or modified activities. (See chapter 1.)

   e. *Report pertinent data.* Develop reporting formats that will keep those directly concerned informed and involved. Use reports for restructuring procedures to meet the stated objectives. (See list of reporting items in the beginning of this section.)

   f. *Diffuse improvements throughout the system.* Establish meetings, task forces and structures to diffuse improvements. Mobile units, in-service work, incentive committees, and every possible stimulating and meaningful activity should be used to bring about change for improvement.

Obtaining Value for Media Dollars

Most school districts have substantially increased their media resources in the past few years. Record players, tape recorders, motion picture projectors, filmstrip machines and TV equipment have increased substantially throughout the country. Many districts now have language labs, educational television facilities, teaching machines, production equipment for making graphics, etc. Media libraries that house films, audio tapes, sets of transparencies and filmstrips are commonplace today.

This increase in resources hopefully implies that better teaching can occur. It also means, almost certainly, greatly increased costs for maintenance and repair of materials and equipment. One way to obtain full media value is to decrease maintenance costs.

Most school districts send their media maintenance and repair work out of the district—to electrical shops, to retail outlets, or to manufacturers. The more electronic equipment purchased and used, the more practical it becomes to undertake maintenance within the district. The employment of a media technician who would be responsible for keeping electronic equipment in top shape, whether he is full or part time, would be an economic asset to the district.

Unfortunately, few places in the country are training educational media technicians. This type of skilled worker would probably have to be recruited from the electronics industry or from the home-repair field to maintain television sets, tape recorders and record players. Manufacturers who sell motion picture projectors, television equipment and other sophisticated items are very cooperative in training new technicians, either in the school district or at their own factories—frequently at their own expense.

A technician need not be a "professional" with a teaching license. He should be able to repair equipment quickly and well as a result of training and experience. For example, retired military personnel should be sought for this particular job. Any potential savings should be measured against his full- or part-time salary, fringe benefits, and the cost of the parts and repair of the equipment he would need, however.

The same technician might also assist in establishing a vocational training program for youngsters, thus utilizing the services of the students in a relevant maintenance program. Of greater importance, the students would receive the practical training necessary for obtaining subsequent employment. If a media maintenance program were to be established as part of the high school electronics department, student enrollment would register marked increases. Many students would be sufficiently advanced to be capable of working with technicians on actual repairs in the electronics area under the overall supervision of their teacher.

There are other reasons for employing a media maintenance technician. He can assist in developing work-study programs, designing recording studios, developing tape-duplicating facilities, and serving on in-service training teams.

Educational technology will continue to advance rapidly in the years ahead. Employing a trained media technician to repair and maintain equipment and to provide other media and instructional services makes good sense. The technician can assist in maintaining a high quality and economical media program.

Beyond cutting maintenance costs there are a number of actions that can be taken to insure the obtaining of value for media dollars.

1. Begin with three basic questions:
    a. Are teachers familiar with the function and operation of the instructional materials and equipment available to them?
    b. Do they use a variety of media equipment and materials effectively?
    c. Do they preview media so that they know what is available and how it may be used in the classroom?
2. Involve teachers in developing an effective evaluation system (see chapter 1).
3. Appoint a media coordinator—full or part time—to establish programs, conduct workshops, and assist teachers in using media to improve instruction.
4. Provide in-service training (see chapter 4).
5. Establish a maintenance program.
6. Seek supplemental funding through federal, state and foundation aid.
7. Coordinate services with other schools and districts to avoid duplication by sharing resources and to provide a greater variety of materials and programs.
8. Investigate the use of media with teaching teams, teacher aides, flexible scheduling, small- and large-group instruction, independent studies, and other organizational and staff differentiation programs to increase quality without increasing cost or to decrease cost at no sacrifice to quality.

How to Recognize Apathy, Blocks and Do-Nothings

Studies on "career-bound" and "place-bound" administrators suggest that confidence, progress, and optimism are more closely associated with the career-bound, while silence is frequently synonymous with the place-bound. Career-bound administrators were much more interested in "action desired" than "personal characteristics desired" factors. Further, the actions sought by the career-bound were primarily those of improving instruction, staff morale, expanding and providing buildings, and developing positive public relations; whereas the place-bound were primarily interested in perpetuating existing programs.[3]

Apathy and progress-blocking are apparently more characteristic of those who achieve promotions in their home districts than of those who move to acquire increases in rank, salary, or status.

Dr. Edgar Dale of Ohio State University discussed "Good Reasons for Doing Nothing" [4] as early as 1945. Frequently people are hesitant about opposing forward-looking proposals, but they can find "good reasons" why new programs cannot be developed or implemented "now." Dr. Dale speculates that many people fear loss of advantage and change itself. They dread insecurity, discomfort, new decision making, and loss of comfortable routines. The do-nothings will offer the following "stand-pat" answers to proposals for change:

1. "The proposal would set a precedent"—or the reverse—"There is no precedent to guide us."
2. "Let's study this awhile; after all, we haven't conclusively proved that the old method can't be made to work or that the proposed new one can."
3. "Let's table it for the next meeting."
4. "It's just another fad. I've seen these bandwagons come and go."
5. "It'll raise taxes!"
6. "The time is not ripe."
7. "We haven't enough data!"
8. "The situation is hopeless."
9. "Why don't we turn this over to a committee?"
10. "We just can't afford it."
11. "We're over-involved as it is! Who's got the time?"
12. "It's too controversial."
13. "It was good enough for my father and it was good enough for me. Why isn't it good enough for my children?"

Recognize the do-nothings quickly and get on with the task of doing something with media to improve teaching and learning.

---

[3] Richard O. Carlson, "Studies Reveal Significant Difference Between Career Bound, Place Bound Superintendents," *Perspectives,* University of Oregon (Spring, 1969).

[4] Edgar Dale, *The News Letter,* Ohio State University (January, 1945), reprinted in *Reel News,* Washington State University (December, 1968).

Using Media to Your Advantage

Media can be used as a powerful tool of persuasion in areas other than teaching. The following examples were taken from actual situations in which media "saved the day."

1. A media specialist in a very conservative district that was having budget troubles utilized a multimedia presentation at a public board of education meeting to effect an increase in equipment and personnel. He succeeded by using slides, a sound track, opaque projection, overhead projection, three screens, and a packet of materials prepared for each board member.
2. An administrator established a media carnival to demonstrate the effectiveness of a countywide federally funded program. Over 200 board of education members came and visited dozens of booths and displays that were manned by consultants and leaders of the projects in the program. Media was in evidence at every turn. More than ninety per cent of those in attendance endorsed the program on returned questionnaires.
3. A media specialist utilized a media fair for PTA meetings. Commercial companies carpeted and brought equipment to the gym. Parents were allowed to use the equipment and materials and were treated to demonstrations of the equipment with students. Support for media was established at each of the fairs.
4. A group of teachers used photographs and 8mm movies of crowded and deplorable conditions to aid a successful bond issue for a new building.
5. An administrator aided in changing yearly "no" votes on the school budget into "yes" by calling public hearings and showing a series of overhead transparencies and 35mm slides to demonstrate needs and justify requests. He utilized a hook and loop board and large colored cards to explain salary increases. A grease pencil and the overhead projector were used effectively to answer questions.
6. A regional center dispelled "centralization" fears among component districts by filming the potential services of a cooperative agency and forwarding the film and a speaker to individual district PTA and board meetings.

Tips on Proposal Writing

Increased competition for funds—federal, state and foundation—and the decreasing supply of money are making it more difficult for local districts to obtain supplemental grants to improve media (or other) programs. The increasing sophistication of proposal readers and the proliferation of guidelines make it more important than ever to observe some fundamental approaches to the development of a sound proposal. Examine one hypothetical situation and determine the right-wrong procedures:

The situation: As an administrator of a racially and economically mixed district, you are concerned about the high dropout rate among black students. Your board, reluctant to appropriate funds for a special project in this year of belt-tightening, suggests that you design an innovative program and submit it for government funding. You set out to do so.

1. *Define the need:* You know, generally, what the problem is and what the general objectives of your proposal will be. In applying for funds, however, you must define the need in terms of *specific* problems and solutions.

It would be very ineffective to rely on *your feelings* about the problem and what you can learn from your associates.

A much more viable procedure would be to go out into the field and discover exactly what the problem is by gathering statistics on who drops out and when (i.e., is the problem primarily in the ninth grade, the tenth grade, or the eleventh grade?). Talk to the people who are directly involved in and affected by the dropout problem. Ask *them* to describe programs that might eliminate or ameliorate the problem. Consult the students themselves to find out *why* they are dropping out.

2. *Develop a plan:* Any major problem, like a high dropout rate, usually contains *many* interrelated problems. For each problem that you define, there are usually several possible solutions, each with a basic set of procedures that should be followed. Your proposal *must* outline specific procedures that solve defined problems in the most efficient way in terms of cost, time and results.

It would be tempting to adopt *your* pet solution to the problem and assume that the agency granting the funds will agree that you are in a position to know the most about the solution required.

It would be much more effective, however, to involve as many as possible in the planning stage. Many of the same people who helped define the problem are in a position to propose solutions. This is especially true of the students who are affected by the proposal. Also, involving as many people as possible is a good way to gain confidence in the proposal you finally do submit.

3. *Write the proposal:* At this point, reverse tactics, and assign the writer or writing team with care.

You may think that you should allow all of your "idea" people to help with the actual drafting of the proposal. The guaranteed result of this approach is a royal smorgasbord that will make everyone happy—except the readers, who will vote "no" on a mélange of ideas.

The more effective procedure would be to appoint only one or two people to write the proposal. They should have been involved in all of the planning, but they should be allowed to do the *writing* without interference. Of course, the draft they submit must conform to what the various planning committees have agreed upon. An explanation of the district's problem should be included in general terms, so that the reader is oriented to the situation before he analyzes the specifics of the proposal.

4. *Research:* Whatever your problem is, you can be almost one hundred per cent certain that your district is not the first to face it. Research tells you what others have already learned and what others have done and *not* done.

Guard against assuming that your problem is so unique, and your proposal so brilliant, that it is in a class by itself.

Be certain that you are *completely* familiar with everything that has been done in the area of your proposal. ERIC (Education Research Information Center) and PACE (Projects to Advance Creativity in Education) can help you learn if anything similar to your program has already been attempted. If so, determine if that project can be adapted to your needs.

5. *Evaluation:* This naturally follows the "completion" of your project.

Remember that evaluation techniques include observing the project as it develops.

You should not advocate standardized tests and other evaluation measures that monitor trends unrelated to the aim of your project. One of the main complaints of funding agencies is that districts too often pretend they will be able to measure the improvement of something like "poor self-image" through a series of standardized reading tests.

Be certain to examine all possible evaluative techniques. Most programs are not going to be conducted by research teams, and funding agencies do not require "scientific" measurements. Interviews, even informal discussions with the people for whom the project is designed, can be valid methods of discovering if a problem is being eased. (See chapter 1.)

6. *Documentation:* If you have done all of the investigation necessary for your project, you should include proof of this in the proposal.

A cover letter, explaining what you did, where you went for information and with whom you spoke is certain to be dry and uninteresting to the readers of your proposal, who see too much of this type of documentation.

Instead, attach an appendix to your proposal. Include copies of letters of commitment from the people who will actually do the *work*. If the plan is to give black students more opportunity for on-the-job experience in offices, stores and factories, attach copies of letters from the management of those businesses stating that they will participate. This demonstrates practical relevance and potential for follow-through.

How to Launch a Media Program from Ground Zero

"I'd really *like* to get an effective media program going in my district, but I can't get it off the ground because we just don't have enough money to hire a director."

This is a familiar lament—and perhaps one with which you can readily identify. What *do* you do when your board or community perennially cuts budgets just at the point where money is requested to hire someone called a "media coordinator"? Is it possible to develop an effective media program without budgeting for an "expert" director? The answer is *yes,* if you really want to begin with what you already have.

Most districts have media materials and equipment. A school can add to its supply of projectors, tape recorders, phonographs, and the software that go with them without ever spending a great deal of money at one time. As for staff, most schools have all the personnel they need to establish and maintain a respectable program—but people do not recognize this.

Even though a part- or full-time trained media coordinator is highly desirable, your budget may not permit the immediate hiring of this specialist. One possible choice then, as overall administrator of a program in each school, is the librarian. Her training in organization, storage and circulation of curriculum materials makes her a potential coordinator. In addition, most librarians are already quite enthusiastic about multimedia materials and anxious to add them to their shelves. These materials can be cataloged right along with the book collection, making them easily accessible to both students and teachers.

Realistically, a librarian cannot be expected to care for projectors, recorders and phonographs as well as perform her normal duties. Maintenance of this equipment requires special knowledge and skills, so you will need a few competent mechanics. A good place to locate such talent is on the faculty of your science department where you will probably find someone who is willing to take on the task—if you provide some help.

Finding that help will probably be the easiest part of setting up the program because you have eager resources in every school—your students. With a faculty member as sponsor, a student media club can do a remarkably capable job of taking care of your expensive equipment. All you have to do is study similar clubs in other districts to see that this is true.

Another school resource person who should be part of a "cooperative" media program is the art teacher. Here is your expert in the use of visuals to make lessons more interesting. A good idea is to allow other teachers time to consult with the artist, who can tell them how to use felt boards, transparencies and other materials to make teaching and learning more exciting.

Once you have identified a team that can provide direction and thrust to a media program, you will have to train the team so that they, in turn, can train teachers to incorporate media into their lessons. There are three good ways to accomplish this:

1. *Establish an In-service Program.* This involves a media specialist to conduct after-school training sessions for your team. A nearby university or college can be an excellent source of appropriate personnel.

2. *Offer Summer Training Sessions.* In many areas, the media coordinator of a neighboring district with a sophisticated media program would conduct a summer program.

3. *Offer College Training.* If possible, offer the leaders of your program an opportunity to take college courses for training as media specialists. Most library schools and teachers' colleges have such programs, and the American Library Association or the Department of Audiovisual Instruction of NEA can supply information on which courses are available.

In the absence of a trained media specialist, the burden of leadership rests with the individual building principals. In their roles as teacher and curriculum evaluators, they are in a unique position to recommend the use of media in the classroom. To meet this responsibility effectively, they must know which materials their school has, where they are stored, and how they can be used. But the new media team and the teaching staff should be involved from the beginning in moving media equipment and materials out of the closets and into the classrooms.

Of critical importance, the media director, the coordinator, the assistant, an aide, or the team should act to translate teaching needs into media presentations; they should be capable of innovating to improve instruction. (See chapter 1, How to Get Started, for details and follow-through.)

Planning the Total Community

In this book it is not possible to do more than touch the surface of the deep and complex societal problems that face us in the decades ahead. The relationships among national goals, education and the use of media for total communications seem obvious, but much needs to be done in planning and developing total communities.

Philadelphia, for example, has instituted a "dispersed" or "parkway school." Instead of planning a new high school, students meet at various locations in the city and report to counselors for assignment to industrial and commercial places of business for learning and working experiences.

New York has plans for a "super block" and "linear city," the first horizontal and the second vertical, to merge all elements of society including education; while Chicago's "magnet schools" were designed around the multi-instructional complex concept of education.

The Everywhere School

Hartford has taken an even bolder step with its "everywhere school" plan. The traditional school would be redesigned and broken up into a series of instructional spaces. Group facilities would be used by students and adults with the library and instructional materials center serving the community as a focal learning area. The auditorium would double as a theater. The first floors of all buildings would be reserved for school areas, stores or recreational facilities. Walking downstairs to a multi-instructional area that could also be used as a recreational den or adult learning space would make the educational process an integral part of the community.

Hartford's "everywhere school" approaches the total solution but seems to rely on random interest and involvement of adults. Much more is needed to integrate the varying facets of society.

Further, educators have become increasingly aware that many children are entering our city and suburban schools with little previous experience in areas that serve to develop skills and abilities necessary as a foundation for academic learning. For example, an inadequately spoken and conceptualized vocabulary prevents successful involvement with reading readiness activities. The lack of basic understandings of time, distance, space, and number concepts serves to widen the gap between exposure and absorption. A traditional kindergarten readiness program is too late and insufficient for children who have not been trained to listen, follow directions, verbalize, interact, and concentrate. When children have additional problems of emotional immaturity, short attention spans, a knowledge of English only as a second language, or an inability to adapt to group situations, it becomes increasingly difficult for them to complete the cognitive requirements of an initial school experience within one year. Preschool, educationally disadvantaged youngsters need to be exposed to an interesting, stimulating, readiness program long before they enter a schoolroom or even a "Head Start" program. The development of "learning-living room" situations for these children would involve adequate preparation for successful academic achievement.

The Living-Room School

One plan that combines community involvement with early childhood education was developed by co-author Tanzman and architect John Shaver.

The plan, entitled "The Living-Room School" (Figures 8–1, 8–2 and 8–3), would have four objectives:

1. preparing disadvantaged preschoolers (two and one-half to five years of age) to ensure "successful" kindergarten experiences. The "curriculum" includes a heavy emphasis on developing verbal and expression skills;

2. training certifiable and certified early-childhood and elementary school teachers to develop and utilize teaching strategies particularly designed for disadvantaged children to provide "successful" kindergarten experiences;

3. training parents whose children participate in the program to understand the philosophy and aims of the Living-Room School and to further strengthen their youngsters' learning experiences; and

Figure 8–1. Apartment buildings housing Living-Room Schools would be rehabilitated outside and in. Exteriors would be distinctive, though not uniform, and children might even have a separate half-sized door. (Designed by Shaver and Company, Architects, Salina, Kansas.)

Figure 8–2. Large spaces in the apartments—usually the living rooms—will be used during the day for indoor play areas. Open space on a dining-room wall might double as a projection screen and the dining area serve as an audience arena. (Designed by Shaver and Company, Architects, Salina, Kansas.)

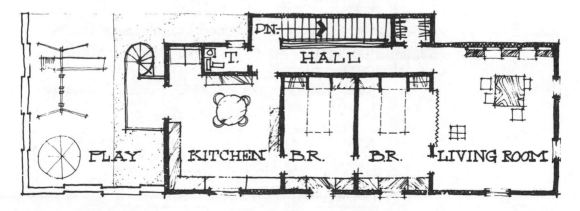

Figure 8–3. Apartments provide the Living-Room School setting; flexibility and convertible furniture serve both the students and residents. Home study units, with audiovisually equipped carrels, would put learning into the neighborhoods and reach out to draw the community into the educational program. (Designed by Shaver and Company, Architects, Salina, Kansas.)

4. training unqualified and uncertified parents as aides in the Living-Room Schools.

The Living-Room School for early-age preschoolers should be expanded to plan for family learning centers within every home or apartment. Home-study media units and cable retrieval systems for family learning tables would further tie the family, the community and the schools together.

These and other proposed solutions for educational problems that are being discussed by boards of city planners and technology specialists are partial at best. The problems of social, economic, political, and total human integration are larger than either a "super block," a "magnet school," or even an "everywhere school."

The Fully Integrated Community

The solutions to educational problems lie in change that can fully integrate not just the schools, but the entire community. (See Figures 8–4 and 8–5.)

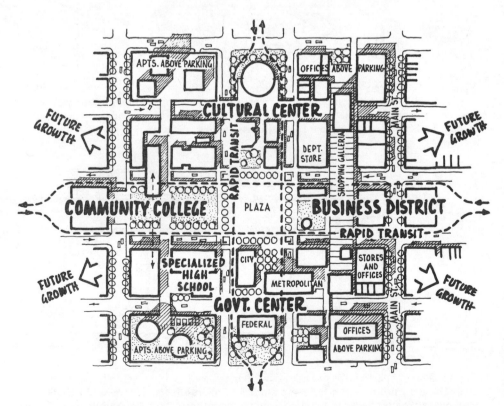

Figure 8–4. Designed by Charles W. Brubaker, Partner, The Perkins and Will Partnership, Architects, Chicago, New York and Washington.

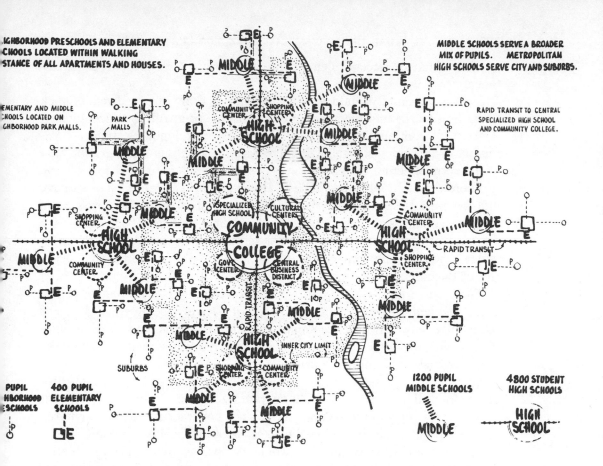

Figure 8–5. No school is an island. Each is related and interrelated. The smallest child walks to his own small preschool, then to a larger (but still small) elementary school, linked by park-malls to other schools, including a larger middle school. Large size means greater mix. The high schools, for both economic and social reasons, are big, serving both city and suburbs, and on rapid transit lines to provide access to a specialized high school (as business and government and retailing) at the city center. The central business district is the good, convenient, interesting, even stimulating location for the community college. The result—a metropolitan system of school facilities, created in response to known social needs. (Designed by Charles W. Brubaker, Partner, The Perkins and Will Partnership, Architects, Chicago, New York and Washington.)

Start by planning a self-contained community, bound and regenerated by a new kind of total educational program. The community's demographic structure would parallel the racial, cultural and economic structure of the country as a whole. Largely self-sufficient, it would be closely tied to the larger community.

This community would provide pleasant and appropriate housing for the poor and for the very wealthy. It would be designed with quiet, traffic-free outdoor surroundings and the privacy necessary for a rewarding family life. Residents might elect or be encouraged to work in the community by

199

guaranteeing easy access to employment in terms of reward and short distance.

Such a community could act as a magnet to draw ex-city dwellers back from the suburbs into the exciting crosscurrents of a truly blended society. As suburbs continue to be absorbed into vast megalopolises, such a community could serve as a stabilizing agent, preventing the out-migration that is currently afflicting the cities.

There is little doubt that much of the current rush from city to suburb, and from established suburb to newer, more distant suburban areas, is in large measure a search for "better" educational systems. Today's parents are willing to make extreme personal sacrifices to place their children in better schools. Many believe these schools can only be found beyond the rim of the cities.

There are other reasons behind the mass retreat, of course. Safety, peace, quiet, and better living conditions are factors. All else being equal, it seems likely that only a truly exceptional educational system, one that is integrated with the total community, will stem the outward flow, bring the escapees back, and improve our society.

Such a school system would encompass prenursery school through programs for senior citizens. It would operate twenty-four hours a day all year round. Instruction would be completely on a nongraded basis and centered largely in the home, involving the latest technological innovations.

The schools in this community would be specifically designed to realize the ideal of education as a lifelong process of growth and change.

Elements of this system would include:

1. Preschool centers located next to or in each high-rise apartment building and within a few minutes' walk of every garden apartment or private home.
2. K–3 schools, each serving 300 pupils.
3. 4–8 schools, each serving 750 pupils.
4. A central 9–12 school coupled with a two-year college, adult education facilities, retraining facilities—the entire unit functioning as a community center.

These schools would operate primarily as resource centers. Most teachers in the system would be subject matter specialists rather than generalists. Comprehensive examinations would permit each student to participate in the development of a curriculum tailored to his individual needs in a basically nongraded system. Every child—every person—would have a different program.

Much of the learning in the lower schools would occur in the school buildings themselves. However, as students develop independent interests and the responsibility to pursue them individually and effectively, they would be encouraged to use educational resources outside the school walls. The offices and shops of the community's small businesses, houses of worship, community services, and light industry would be among these resources.

The fully equipped special learning centers in each apartment building and automated study centers located in each home would be central to the learning process.

The learning centers in each apartment building would be located on a recreation and education floor open to all occupants of the building—not just to "students." In addition to a gymnasium and a swimming pool, the area would include a small library (paperbacks, magazines, programed materials, reference books) and ample spaces for lectures, concerts and meetings. Equipment in the center would include closed-circuit television connecting the viewer to the schools and—through a centrally located computer system—a host of instructional materials.

The home study center—a corner, a closet, or an entire room—would be connected directly to the schools and the central computer. These areas would make home study far less isolated by permitting students to deal directly with their teachers via preprogramed instruction fed into the computer and retrieved at will with the aid of a simple control panel. Each study center would be equipped with easy-to-operate media aids; audio and video tapes, filmstrips, films, records, and slides would be available in the building's library. Both hardware and software could be checked out for use in the home.

This home study center would be a resource for everyone in the family. Children would use it for recreational purposes as well as for study. Parents would use it for job retraining, work on advanced degrees or "in-service" vocational and professional training. Education would become a lifelong, never-ending process for everyone.

Education, of course, should not be restricted to the home or to the immediate home environment. Consequently, the community would house a large cultural center in the high-school–college complex that would be designed for continuous educational and entertainment activities. Such a center would include an art gallery, a hall for the performing arts, a miniature museum, housing exhibits on loan from major museums in the country, and arts and crafts studios open to every member of the community.

Like the schools, the cultural center would be open twenty-four hours a day for 365 days a year. It, too, would house many recreational facilities, such as tennis courts, not included in the recreation and education centers of the community's individual dwellings.

The social organization would provide racial and economic integration. Housing in the community would range from superior low-rent dwellings that most employees could afford to middle-class garden apartments, duplex homes, and the most lavishly appointed cooperative apartment-homes. These would be arranged so that residents of varying income strata might conceivably live side by side. They could pass each other in the lobbies of their apartment buildings, in the elevators, in the schools, in their building's recreation and education center, and in the churches and temples located close by. In all probability, they would never speak to each other but that would not be detrimental. It is not anticipated that adults of disparate economic and social groups will necessarily become fast friends (they probably would not). Of importance is the concept that their children all have equally enriching educational, recreational, and social opportunities. The effect of enrichment would not be felt immediately but would become apparent in future generations.

Integration implies working together as well as meeting, learning and playing together. This community would offer many opportunities for social and economic integration. Shopping centers, laundries, repair shops, and a motel-hotel-restaurant complex would provide numerous service jobs. Professionals—health, education and welfare specialists—would have office space in a community professonal building. Light industry would create both blue- and white-collar employment as well as executive positions.

These industries would complement the educational program by providing valuable cooperative educational experiences for the community's youngsters. The educational system would reciprocate by providing specific job training for future employees. Skills training centers would be located within the industries themselves and connected to the educational program via closed-circuit television and work-study programs. The central computer would provide upgrading and retraining instruction for study in these centers; it would also be available for systems analysis, accounting, stock control, and other forms of evaluation and appraisal.

In summary, the fully integrated community would have these advantages:

—The outstanding educational and enrichment opportunities would attract some middle- and upper-class residents (who would not ordinarily move into a "housing development"). Extremely reasonable rentals that are carefully controlled would attract low-income families.

—A large reservoir of employables, services and educational facilities would attract and hold light industry, thus providing a solid economic foundation for the entire community.

—For those who enjoy community living—and many people do—it

would represent a fairly accurate cross section of our society working at optimum capacity in an essentially democratic fashion.

Can America afford to offer less to its future citizens?

SELECTED BIBLIOGRAPHY AND
SOURCES OF ADDITIONAL INFORMATION
ON MEDIA INSTRUCTION

Anderson, Charnel, *History of Instructional Technology. I: Technology of American Education, 1650–1900,* Occasional Paper No. 1. Washington, D.C.: National Education Association, Department of Audiovisual Instruction, December 1964. 53 pp. Also published by (and order from) Office of Education, Washington, D.C.: Government Printing Office, 1962. 53 pp.

Audiovisual Market Place. New York: R. R. Bowker Company, 1969. (A directory of the audiovisual industry.)

Audio Visual Source Directory. Tarrytown, New York: Motion Picture Enterprises Publications, Inc. (Published semi-annually.)

Brown, James W., Lewis, Richard B., and Harcleroad, Fred F., *A-V Instruction: Materials and Methods* (2nd ed.). New York: McGraw-Hill Book Co., 1964. 592 pp.

Dale, Edgar, *Audio-Visual Methods in Teaching* (3rd ed.). New York: Holt, Rinehart & Winston, 1965. 534 pp.

deKieffer, Robert, and Cochran, Lee W., *Manual of Audio-Visual Techniques* (2nd ed.). Englewood Cliffs, N.J.: Prentice-Hall, Inc., 1961. 254 pp.

Diamond, Robert M., editor, *A Guide to Instructional Television.* New York: McGraw-Hill Book Co., 1964. 314 pp.

Educational Communications Handbook. Albany: New York State Education Department, Division of Educational Communications, 1968.

"Educational Technology." Washington, D.C.: National Education Department, Division of Educational Technology. (Pamphlet published periodically.)

Ely, Donald, editor, "The Changing Role of the Audiovisual Process in Education: A Definition and a Glossary of Related Terms." Supplement No. 6. *AV Communication Review* 11:1–148; January–February 1963. 148 pp. (Order directly from Johnson Reprint Corporation, 111 Fifth Avenue, New York City 10003.)

Engelhardt, N. L., *Complete Guide for Planning New Schools.* West Nyack, N.Y.: Parker Publishing Co., 1970.

Erickson, Carlton W. H., *Fundamentals of Teaching with Audiovisual Technology.* New York: The Macmillan Co., 1965. 384 pp.

Goodwin, Arthur B., *Handbook of Audio-Visual Aids and Techniques for Teaching Elementary School Subjects*. West Nyack, N.Y.: Parker Publishing Co., 1969.

Kemp, Jerrold E., *Planning and Producing Audiovisual Materials* (2nd ed.). San Francisco: Chardler Publishing Co., 1968.

Lewis, Philip, *Educational Television Guidebook*. New York: McGraw-Hill Book Co., 1961. 238 pp.

Limbacher, James L., *Using Films*. New York: Education Film Library Association, 1967.

Mialaret, G., *The Psychology of the Use of Audio-Visual Aids in Primary Education*. New York: UNESCO, 1966. (There are many UNESCO publications in this area.)

Minor, E. O., *Simplified Techniques for Preparing Visual Instructional Materials*. New York: McGraw-Hill Book Co., 1962. 136 pp.

Palovic, Lora, and Goodman, Elizabeth, *The Elementary School Library in Action*. West Nyack, N.Y.: Parker Publishing Co., 1968.

Rufsvold, Margaret I., and Guss, Carolyn, *Guides to Newer Education Media* (2nd ed.). Chicago: American Library Association, 1967.

Schultz, Morton J., *The Teacher and Overhead Projection*. West Nyack, N.Y.: Parker Publishing Co., 1965.

Scuorzo, Herbert, *Practical Audio-Visual Handbook for Teachers*. West Nyack, N. Y.: Parker Publishing Co., 1967.

Standards for School Media Programs. Chicago: American Library Association, and Washington: National Education Association, 1969. 66 pp.

Steig, Lester R., and Frederick, E. Kemp, *School Personnel and In-Service Training Practices*. West Nyack, N.Y.: Parker Publishing Co., 1969.

Thomas, R. Murray, and Swartout, Sherwin G., *Integrated Teaching Materials* (rev. ed.). New York: McKay, 1963. 559 pp.

Weisgerber, Robert A., editor, *Instructional Process and Media Innovation*. Chicago: Rand McNally & Co., 1968.

Wittich, Walter A., and Schuller, Charles, *Audio-Visual Materials: Their Nature and Use* (3rd ed.). New York: Harper and Row, Publishers, Inc., 1962. 500 pp.

Index